REPUBLIC

The author of this book is a long time republican
who lives and works in England.

REPUBLIC

The case against the monarchy

ANONYMOUS

Copyright © Anonymous 2014

All rights reserved. No part of this publication may be reproduced, stored in a retrieval system, or transmitted in any form or by any means, electronic, mechanical, photocopying, recording, or otherwise, without the prior permission of both the copyright owner and the publisher of this book.

This book is dedicated to all of those men and women throughout history who have battled against tyranny, in whatever form it took, both evil and benign, and whose words, writings, and statements we will remain enlightened by for many years to come, and without whom this book would not have been possible.

CONTENTS

INTRODUCTION

Of the various forms of government which have
prevailed in the world, an hereditary monarchy
seems to present the fairest scope for ridicule.
- Edward Gibbon

As I write this paragraph, in the early summer of 2014, the following is the case; we have landed men on the moon, we have developed nuclear power in the form of fission and are close to working out the problems of nuclear fusion, we have built the largest and most complex machine ever made by human hands and minds in the Large Hadron Collider, and have used it to find out things about the nature of reality that we could scarcely have guessed at. We have developed the scientific method which is the best way, so far, of uncovering the mysteries of the universe, we have built a global civilisation that for all its faults means that wars and conflicts are far less common than they should be (given that we are only a chromosome or two away from chimpanzees), and we know much more, and simultaneously much less, about the universe and our place in it than we ever have done in the history of mankind. So, it may seem strange that we, in the United Kingdom and some other parts of the world at least, cling to a method of government that can be called, without exaggeration, primitive. Who would have thought, that with all of the hard won attainments that our ancestors strived and battled for, that we would still toil under a system that rewards bloodline and not merit, tradition instead of progression, and superstition instead of enlightenment. To date the monarchy has not been critiqued as much as its claims warrant that it should be, and this could be said to be the peoples original sin, for only with examination, then critique, then ridicule, can an edifice as imposing and seemingly impenetrable as the monarchic system be overthrown. This pamphlet is my case against monarchy and against the right of humans to rule over each other by automatic right. I hope I can show that this right does not exist, and contrarily that the right of any human to pursue life, liberty, and happiness, is, as in the words of that great humanist Thomas Jefferson, self evident.

Part I

The critique

CHAPTER 1

The first King

> I have friends in overalls whose friendship I would
> not swap for the favour of the kings of the world.
> - Thomas Edison

In the United Kingdom we all know about the current royal family and their goings on, whether we want to or not, but the history of how kings and queens came to be is not so well understood. Logic dictates that if there are such things as kings and queens, then there must have been a first king or queen, but there are many questions that arise once this premise has been accepted. How did that king or queen come to power? Why did they believe they had a right to rule? Why did the general populace accept the outcome? Did they accept it without question? Were there some at the time who did not accept it, and what happened to those who did question the monarch? We also know that kings and queens claim to the throne is hereditary, but when did this claim originate, and with whom?

I would be the first to admit that in the early days of human society, men would have been feudal in nature. This is to be expected, as after all, we are only mammals, and mammals have all sorts of undesirable traits that force them into conflict with each other. Battles over food, land, women, and many other factors would have no doubt been very prominent in the early childhood of our species, and I expect they will be around for a long time to come. It would not have been possible, in my opinion at least, for the sort of society that we are striving for to have been possible five hundred years ago, let alone a thousand. In fact, we cannot even do it now, as advanced as we are. It could be very well argued that the primitive society that existed would have needed an ultimate ruler; someone who could unite all of the warring tribes under one banner, and bring about some semblance of civility. The methods used to put this ruler in place, and to keep them there once they were in power, would not have been reasonable, it is safe to assume. Blood would have been shed, skulls would have been cracked, and land and property would have been seized without mercy or risk of punishment. So, who was the first king? The answer, if we go back far enough, would possibly be Alulim, who is believed to have been the first king of Sumer, and the first human ever proclaiming himself to be what we would understand as a king. Many other men and women throughout history have named themselves divine and above all others, and listing the names of all of those people and understanding the interplay between them would be impossible, and perhaps futile. For our critique, all we need to know is that at all times and in all places, men and women have proclaimed themselves king or queen, and as a result, held positions of power over the common man. Whether they did this for their own greed or the well being of others is impossible to state with certainty, but it would be wise to assume that there would have been men and women who came down on both sides of the divide.

It has been said that without kings and queens there may not have been the advances in society that were so desperately needed at the time. This I would be inclined to agree with, if only because it is at least a credible argument. Alfred the Great, who ruled Wessex originally before incorporating all of England into his realm, did many things that could be considered progressive even by todays standards. He was apparently a learned man, who encouraged education, improved the legal and military systems, and also strived to improve the lives of his subjects. He also repelled the Vikings numerous times, so it seems like we are in his debt, at least to some degree. It is not too outrageous then, to state that the first kings and queens would undoubtedly have been the most intelligent, most cunning, most charismatic, most persuasive, and strongest individuals in the society in which they dwelled. We can learn a lot about how this would have come to be by simply looking at other mammal groups, and more specifically, primate mammal groups. It is nearly always the biggest and strongest Silverback Gorilla who becomes the leader of the troop, and acts to protect the more vulnerable members from harm. We as humans have an obviously more advanced social structure, but the basic premise is the same. The most powerful person, whether it was agreed by society as a whole or not, normally took power for themselves and then kept it by force, fear, or a combination of the two. Whether kings and queens believed that they were more powerful naturally would be open to doubt, but my opinion is that they would have to have done. We see huge egos and inflated self confidence in film stars and sports stars in our modern society, and many of them do what they can to bribe, blackmail, and bully those around them into submission. However, we do not live in the middle ages anymore. We do not live in a feudal society, and we do not need an antiquated method of government that has no real benefits either for the people who are trapped within its ranks (the members of the royal family themselves) and those who are deemed to be the subjects of said family. Is it really too cheap a point to say that we do not need their help anymore, and that we would be better off without them?

Another very important facet of monarchy and kingship is religion, which kings and queens have always allied themselves with, for the obvious reasons. The Roman philosopher Lucius Annaeus Seneca was recorded as saying that; "religion is regarded by the common man as true, by the wise as false, and by the rulers as useful". If the ancient Romans were aware of this, then it is safe to assume that the first kings and queens would have been as well. You are free to believe, if you so wish, that the early kings did not exploit the credulousness and ignorance of the common man and woman, and did not threaten them with hellfire and eternal torment if they did not bow the knee, but it is my opinion that this not only would *have* happened, I do not think kingship would have gained a foothold if it had *not* happened. It is not hard to imagine why the vast majority of people accepted the premise of a king, or someone divinely appointed to rule over them without question. The vast majority of people in prehistory were uneducated, illiterate, and fearful of most things, such as the weather, disease, and all other manner of terrifying and unexplained phenomena. It is also safe to assume that even the most uneducated person today knows far more than the average person who lived in the middle ages. It would be perhaps unfair to say that the populace then needed a ruler, but the more I think about it the more I would be inclined to agree. As has been said, the mob needs a ruler and the ruler needs a mob.

A harder question to answer would be whether every singe member of the public accepted the premise that the king was divinely appointed to rule over them, or accepted that the figure of their king was valid at all. I think that if these views did exist in the early years of our society, they were not common, and they were certainly not wide spread. It seems obvious that the monarch would have done everything in his or her power to quash such thoughts at the source, but again, it is not clear to me that we have anything like convincing evidence for this. An analogy can be made with reference to numerous passages in the bible that state, "the fool hath said in his heart that there is no God". The authors must have surely been talking about men and women that they knew, or at least men and women that were alive at the time they were putting the texts together, so it would not be outrageous to conclude that unbelievers have existed in all places and at all times. We would not have to make a very big leap to come to the conclusion that if there were men and women who did not accept the revelation of God to man, then there must have been some who denied the divine right of kingship, and of the act of one man or woman ruling over them. Alas, there is no definitive way to know how many minds thought this way, and there never will be. It is enough to know that there have always been sceptics, and the best that we can do is to make sure that their objections and voices do not die out with our generation.

To conclude, it is plain to me that the reasons for there being a king or queen might have been valid in the first place, but they are not anymore. Yes, we are a troubled species, and we fight over land, resources, ideology, food, and have many other petty squabbles, but the installation of a dictator who believes himself or herself to be divinely appointed will not and cannot solve these problems, no matter how much we might like to believe to the contrary. We must realise that the only way to progress as a species is to face up to the fact that we are alone in the universe, and to tackle the problems that we are presented with by the only way that works; by using our reason and our scepticism. This, in my view, is flatly negated by the belief that there are higher powers, even human ones, and instead teaches us to think credulously instead of critically.

CHAPTER 2

A divine right to rule

"There is not one redeeming feature in our superstition of Christianity. It has made one half the world fools, and the other half hypocrites."
- Thomas Jefferson

As we have now determined that kings and queens would have come to power by virtue of their strength, intelligence, cunning, influence, charisma, and wealth, we will now examine the way in which they asserted and held onto this power. It would seem that a king would need a very good reason to be in the position he was in, and it would also follow that this reason must resonate with the general public at large. It may surprise you to know that there *is* only one reason, and it may surprise you even more to know that this reason is not put forward as an argument anymore. I am talking about the divine right to rule, also known as the divine right of kingship. To flesh out the background to this it is important to know exactly when, where, and why this divine right to rule originated, and why it is now no longer (publicly at any rate) affirmed.

The theory of the divine right of kings has been around for a very long time, but came to the forefront of theological thinking during the reign of James I of England (1603-1625). In essence, it states that a monarch is subject to no earthly authority, deriving the right to rule directly from God. In other words, the creator handpicks the men and women he wants to rule. The divine right of kingship effectively means that only God can judge an unjust king or queen. If we logically follow this through to its conclusion then it does not matter how odious his or her rule is, or how heinous his or her acts are whilst in power, the people cannot enforce their will on him or her. This then follows that the king or queen could commit unspeakable acts of evil, and then that there would be no man or woman alive who could question those acts. If we strip this concept down to its bare bones, it is in effect saying that the knowledge of a right action or a wrong action can only be affirmed by the creator. This is patently false, and I will invite you to join me in a thought experiment to prove it. Let's say that we read two supposedly moral instructions from the bible; the first that if you find your young bride to be a non-virgin on your wedding night that you must stone her to death on her fathers doorstep, and the second that you should love your neighbour as thyself. You will no doubt have already decided which of these pearls of ancient wisdom is right or wrong morally, but how did you come to this decision? My bet is that it was not by divine revelation, but more simply, you applied your reason and your critical thinking faculties and decided, entirely by yourself, that it is a bad idea to stone your betrothed to death for the non-crime of having sex with someone else before you, and that it is a good idea to extend friendship and love to those around you, even if they are not members of your immediate family.

For an atheist like myself it is actually genuinely offensive that another human being, or in this case, a family of human beings, believe and announce that they alone are divinely appointed to rule over me. It is one thing to believe that the universe and everything in it was created so you could be here, as is the Christian view, but another entirely to think that the creator then personally picked you and your extended family to rule over the rest of the population with impunity. This goes way beyond simple minded solipsism, and moves to a level of arrogance that you would be hard pressed to find in any other human institution. The idea of one person or human mammal being above another is, alas, an all too common theme throughout history, and I challenge anyone to think of a society or civilisation that became better once a human or group of humans were placed above all others. This is bad enough even if the general populace does not believe it to be so, as is the case with most despotic dictatorships, but surely it is much more intolerable if the people themselves are colluding with the leader and making a rod for their own backs.

The reason that the divine right of kingship would have been useful, especially if we think about it in terms of an era of very high illiteracy, superstition, and religious barbarism, is that it then becomes much easier to convince your audience that you are telling the truth. Credulity and ignorance have always been exploited by those who are willing to exploit the credulous and ignorant, which is a fact that is unfortunately not going to change anytime soon. It is hard to imagine, for me at any rate, exactly how superstitious those unfortunate men and women were in the childhood of our civilisation. Priests and other holy men have always been looked up to by the common man, in times of plenty and in times of need. It is no coincidence that many religions now serve as a community function, even if the leaders of those institutions do not really personally believe what they tell their congregations. One can only guess what it must have been like then, to have a man calling himself king, who seemed to be invested with some heavenly authority, flanked by lesser holy men, garbed in gold and furs and other trinkets, speaking eloquently, reading effortlessly, standing tall and regal, and assuring everyone that God put him in charge.

Thomas Paine, writing in *Rights of Man*, said that, "There was a time when kings disposed of their crowns by will upon their deathbeds, and consigned the people, like beasts of the field, to whatever successor they appointed." The great Paine was both right and wrong with this statement, in that crowns did pass down, father to son and mother to daughter, but wrong in the fact that he begun his sentence with the words, "There was a time…". That is the way that succession works *now*, let alone more than two centuries ago when Paine wrote his pamphlet. He may have hoped, or even thought, that at the time of writing the British monarchy was soon to be overthrown, and I think he would be aghast to discover that the despotism endures to this very day.

For the monarchist that maintains that the divine right to rule is now no longer put forward as an argument, we need only look to the royal motto as proof that this statement is vacuous. The royal motto reads *Dieu et mon droit*, which translates as *God and my right*. What are we to think of a group of people, and more specifically a single family or bloodline, that believe themselves to be appointed by the creator of the universe to rule over the rest of us? I could never think myself divinely appointed, not just because I do not think that I was put here by a supernatural entity, but because it would be cringe inducing if I did think so. Who could have the arrogance to think such a thing, let alone announce it, and then show their face in public and feel no shame? I have tried, but I simply cannot imagine Prince Charles coming face to face with Stephen Hawking or Lawrence Krauss or any of the other men and women that strive to understand the universe as it actually is, and not be left slightly red-cheeked. If the divine right of kingship does not now apply, would you not think it prudent to change the motto of the royal house? I leave the question open to you.

It is not possible to know exactly when the divine right of kingship was abandoned, because there may have been, and perhaps certainly were, people who kept the idea lodged in their own minds, and dared not utter it on pain of torture or death. The Glorious Revolution of 1688 certainly put an end to the idea of divine right in many peoples minds, but the theory obviously must still persist, if only in private. When the divine right to rule really became a truly ridiculous proposition was during the rise of the enlightened minds of the American and French revolutions. Thomas Paine, that great, unsung (at least in my own country) writer and polemicist, was the first to put forward the idea that if there was such a thing as the divine right of kings, then there must be such a thing as rights. If there was such a thing as rights, then why didn't everyone have them? Once this thought had entered the minds of the people, and once the question had escaped from their mouths, it could not be unthought or unasked. It seems normal now, but this idea was revolutionary at the time, and Paine and other great thinkers no doubt helped to ridicule and overthrow the theory of the divine right of kingship.

A further problem with the theory arises when we consider what it means when people marry into the royal family. The most recent example of this was when Catherine Middleton, known as Kate Middleton in the media, married Prince William. The question that has to be asked is this; does God now think *her* divinely appointed to rule, if the task so arises? And does Catherine Middleton believe, now that she has married into the right family of course, that she has a divine right to rule? What if she had not married Prince William but had instead married a normal member of the public? Would the creator of the universe then have overlooked her suitability to rule over the rest of us, even though presumably her personality, moral character, and other qualities would be much the same? Again, these simple questions strike the supporters of the monarchy dumb and make laughable the divine theory of kingship.

To summarise, the question that needs to be asked of our present monarch, or to all of them for that matter, is whether or not they truly believe that they have a divine right to rule. By divine I mean granted by God, and by God I mean the Christian God, and even more specifically, the Anglican one. That the creator of the universe should trouble himself or herself (or *itself* potentially), with the banal goings on of an imperfectly evolved primate species on a tiny rock in the middle of a mediocre galaxy, is almost too much for the rational mind to bear. To then think that he, she, or it could then deem it wise to give the right to rule to only one family of a primate mammal species has a long way to go before it's even naive. But this is the situation in which we, in the the United Kingdom and many other countries around the world, find ourselves in. Now you may say that the divine right of kingship has been abandoned, but how do you know this? Has a reigning monarch ever been asked the question? Even if they said no, how can anyone be certain that they do not think it in private, not held down by any earthly laws and not answerable to any either? If the head of state were to one day announce that they were not divinely appointed to rule, then *quo warranto*, by what right do they rule?

CHAPTER 3

Defender of the faith

"In the affairs of the world, men are saved not by faith, but by the lack of it."
- Benjamin Franklin

Now that we have looked at the reasons that kings and queens came into their power, and the reason that they affirmed their position, it is time to examine the actual job title or job description that is assigned to the head of state, at least in the traditional sense. Not many people know what the official job title is for the monarch, but on paper it has been *Defender of the Faith* since 1591, when Pope Leo X appointed the title to Henry VIII (Christopher Hitchens famously said that the absurdity of the royal family is what happens when you found a church with the family values of the aforementioned king). I for one did not know that faith, or belief without evidence, needed defending, and surely if there did need to be such a position, it would be more than a one man job. It is perhaps too obvious to point this out in these days of our more or less secular society, but in the middle ages interfaith warfare and strife would have been high on the agenda of things to be worried about.

It is worth examining exactly what faith is before we start our critique properly. Faith, in the traditional sense of the word, is a religious term, normally used to mean that the person in question believes something with no evidence to back up their claims, or more simply, belief without, or in the face of evidence. It is easy to see how a phenomenon such as faith came to be so prevalent in the human species, especially in a world where nothing was really explained, and many things would have been mysterious and frightening. The men who found a way to explain these phenomena, whether natural or otherwise, would have been at a distinct advantage. If you are a shrewd person, and discover that some event always precedes a future event, such as a rainstorm or natural disaster, then you have power over the people that have not discovered this. It is easy to see how this could have morphed into what we see as modern religion today. Priests, bishops, and other holy men and women claim to know the exact rituals, propitiations, and actions required in this life, and also the rules about reward and punishment in the proposed life to come. This system needs people who have faith. If not, then their authority would be questioned, and then that certainty would turn to doubt, and then that doubt would lead them away from the religion. This situation is the case in the present day, so what must it have been like for those wretches in the dark ages, when not believing or even questioning some of the pronouncements of the holy would have been met with swift and terrible punishment, not just in this world but the next? I sometimes think that we all forget what it is like to live in a society where you can believe whatever you want, and are not forced to adopt some world view on the word of another human, who knows no more about the universe than you do. Faith, in essence, is the polar opposite of everything that is needed for a successful society. I have thought about this long and hard and will phrase it thus: faith has the answer before it has asked the question; reason has the question before it attempts the answer. The difference between these two world views is black and white in my opinion, and anyone that declares otherwise is simply fooling themselves. Faith, whether you like to admit it or not, plays a huge role in many peoples lives, but this does not automatically mean it should be respected. What are we to think of a person that believes the same thing on Monday and Friday, regardless of what happened on the Wednesday? Christopher Hitchens famously said that faith is not a virtue, but if it was, it would be the most overrated of the virtues. Having faith is all well and good, and I will defend the religious persons right to think as they will until my last breath, but in return they must keep their illusions private.

The royal house has, unfortunately, had a long and enduring relationship with religion, which in its many guises has been a blot on the progression of mankind for untold centuries. The English church that we recognise today has gone through a number of schisms and reformations, and it is worth knowing a little of the history behind this. The Church of England became separate from the Roman Catholic church in 1534 after a dispute over the annulment of Henry VIII's marriage to Catherine of Aragon. The Roman church then was brought back in to power over the English church in 1555 during the reign of Mary I and King Philip, but was then rejected again after the rise of Queen Elizabeth I and the Act of Supremacy 1558. Understandably, and as all religions can be relied upon to do, both Catholic and reformist factions fought for control of the specific doctrines that would be adopted by the church. This battle was ended later that year, with the 1558 Elizabethan Settlement, which stated that the church would be both Catholic and Reformed.

Fast forward a few hundred years, and even though society has made numerous progressions, both ethically and morally, the church that enjoys the full support of the state still cannot keep up with what ordinary people find good moral behaviour. An example is the continuing "debate" surrounding the ordination of women and homosexuals. The objection is not well reasoned, or well argued, because it cannot be. The holy books and the texts themselves objectify women and class them no better than chattel, and homosexuality is condemned as a sin in many religions, not just the Christian one. Theologians often ignore the textual and biblical warrants for their objections, and instead try and bring the argument into the modern day, sometimes arguing that homosexuality does not occur in nature, for example. This is patently false, as numerous studies have demonstrated, and just goes to show the lengths to which some people will go to affirm their unfounded beliefs on others.

The Anglican church is often seen as the most mild and timid of all of the different versions of Christianity, and to the outsider it certainly seems like this might be the case. Upon closer inspection, however, it becomes apparent that this view is false. The most recent Archbishop of Canterbury, Rowan Williams, has said that muslims should be allowed sharia law in the UK, as to help solve disputes in their own communities. Never mind that many of the tenets of Islam are flatly incompatible with western civilisation and human rights, especially female human rights; what is the head of the Church of England doing announcing that another religious group should be free to abide by whichever laws they deem suitable? No muslim leader had demanded this, but here was ecumenicism in its most dangerous form. We must remember that the barbarians never take the city until the gates are opened, and they are always opened from the inside. It is my view that this sort of interfaith appeasement is simply a threat to our civilisation, whether you acknowledge it or not. Unfortunately, Rowan Williams is not the only Archbishop of Canterbury to spout utter nonsense when it comes to the realm of religion. Geoffrey Fisher, who was appointed in 1945 and was head of the church until 1961, stated, about nuclear war, that:

> "The very worst the bomb can do is to sweep a vast number of people from this world into the next, into which they all must go anyway."

This, at first glance, looks like it could have been said by any reactionary or fundamentalist person of faith, and you may find it incredible to learn that it did not come from some fanatic or other. It is not surprising to me however, as the wish for this world to be over and done with is at the heart of all the major religions, but surely it is much worse coming from the supposed head of a church for which we pay.

The next in line to the throne, and therefore the next in line to become the head of the Church of England, Prince Charles, has remarked that he wishes to not just be Defender of *the* faith, but Defender of Faith, no doubt hoping to seem as inclusive and progressive as possible in our modern society. He seems to have forgotten however, that many people, myself included, do not believe in a supernatural dimension, and do not believe that a creative intelligence made the universe and everything in it, in order to supervise one imperfectly evolved primate species. He is also seemingly only doing this because of the huge numbers of different religions now flourishing in this country. It is interesting to note that had we been having this discussion in the middle ages, the mere mention of being inclusive to other denominations of Christianity, let alone other faiths altogether, or no faith at all, would have been met with the harshest of penalties. This ecumenicism is not harmless, even if at first glance it seems like it might be. Prince Charles has also made many speeches concerning religion, but one of the most interesting and enlightening paragraphs of just one of these was about the place of faith in the modern world:

> "…today the Middle East and North Africa has the lowest concentration of Christians in the world - just four per cent of the population and it is clear that the Christian population has dropped dramatically over the last century and is falling still further. **This has an effect on all of us, although of course primarily on those Christians who can no longer continue to live in the Middle East. We all lose something immensely and irreplaceably precious when such a rich tradition dating back 2,000 years begins to disappear.**" (emphasis mine)

Of course, Prince Charles is either too ignorant or too stupid to realise that Christians, Muslims, and any other religious group would be perfectly at home in the Middle East, if the governments and regimes there were democratic republics with secular constitutions. As it stands, the religious groups that call the birthplace of Christianity their home are busy fighting amongst each other over the title deeds to the land in question. The Jews were promised the holy land by God, but the problem is, so were the Muslims. They both seem to agree that the creator of the universe deals in real estate, but they simply disagree on which tribe should hold the deeds. Again, the statement that the Middle East would be a poorer place without religion, by the man that will one day become our head of the state, head of the church, and head of the armed forces, is too ridiculous to even bother rebutting. Is there a person alive today that does not think that a mass outbreak of secularism would not make the Middle East a far more plural, diverse, and prosperous place? The question answers itself.

So, if we cannot rid ourselves of a monarchy, and they have to have something to do and an official job title, surely we can come up with something better than *Defender of the Faith*? I will use this space to propose some of my own. How about *Defender of Free Speech*, or *Defender of Reason*, or *Defender of Human Rights*? Reason, intelligence, enlightenment and the other traits of a progressive human society are surely much more important to defend if we wish to build a truly successful and plural system, but it is obvious, after a moments analysis, why this will never be the case. The methods of free inquiry, scepticism, and enlightenment values flatly negate an archaic system such as monarchy almost by definition. Once you grant that humans are free and have certain rights that are unalienable, the principles of heredity and succession and the divine right by which they enforce them become null and void.

This country may have been founded on Christian values, but these days it is very much secular. You may not like to think this is true, but it simply is. This is to the annoyance of many people, even some our politicians. One name that springs to mind is the ridiculous persona of Baroness Warsi, who actually said that Britain was under attack from a virulent strain of "militant secularism" that religious people of all stripes should fight against. She seemingly does not know what "militant", and more importantly "secular" mean. I could go on at length about this, but will condense into a couple of sentences. Simply put, a secular society is one that has the most freedom, not just of religion, but *from* religion. Baroness Warsi doesn't seem to realise that even the most religious person on the planet would benefit from a completely secular government. This is because, by definition, a secular government cannot intervene in religious affairs. Thomas Jefferson phrased this perfectly, in his *Notes on the State of Virginia*, when he opined that:

> "I care not whether my neighbour believes in one hundred gods, one god, or none, by that he neither breaks my bones nor picks my pocket".

To have an official state religion has always struck me as fatuous, as it evidently means that those who do not belong to that particular religion are ostracised right away. This fact would not have been too problematic a few hundred years ago, when it would have been very rare to find a sceptic, and even rarer, perhaps impossible, to find any person that would admit that they doubted the validity of the claims of the religious, let alone that they doubted the existence of a creator. It has only become clear, in my view at least, that this situation has become insufferable in the light of the fact that many people in our society, myself included, do not think that there is a supernatural dimension, that the universe was not created but evolved, and that even if there were an intelligent entity responsible for all that we see, that that entity does not and would not involve itself in the daily life of humans.

In closing, I would like to ask the present or future monarch the following question: do you defend my right to unbelief? If the answer to this question is yes, then surely it makes a mockery of the whole concept of the job title *Defender of the Faith*, and if the answer is no, then what sort of society is it that we have built, where my right to think as I will is not protected by the very people who have placed themselves in the ultimate position of power?

CHAPTER 4

The problem with heredity

The vanity and presumption of governing beyond the grave, is the most ridiculous and insolent of all tyrannies.

- Thomas Paine: *Rights Of Man*

Having now looked at the rise of the first kings and queens, and the ways in which they seized and held onto power, and the specific reasons for them being in the position they are in, it is now time to examine my main objection to the continuation of the monarchy. I am talking of course about the principle of heredity. Thomas Paine, that great Englishman, who despite his tremendous contribution to the human species languishes in anonymity, especially in this country, once remarked that a hereditary ruler makes as much sense as a hereditary doctor or mathematician. He was of course right, in that what does birth have to do with any ability, implied or otherwise, of a particular person to perform a task? The doctor goes to medical school for years and studies long and hard to be able to diagnose and treat numerous diseases. The mathematician goes to university, studies theorems and problems for countless hours and hones his craft. But what of the monarch? They are born into a family, by sheer chance, and this apparent coincidence means that they become head of state of not just these islands, but many other territories as well. Logic and reason balk at such nonsense.

Paine's main reason, and my own, for wanting the monarchy abolished is also the very reason that it endures. Heredity can be simply defined as the passing down of acquired characteristics. However, those traits are much more likely to be purely biological, as opposed to the passing down of mental or moral traits. Simply put, if your grandfather and grandmother were tall and had blonde hair, one of your parents would be much more likely to be tall and have blonde hair, and by extension, you will also have an increased chance of having those characteristics. The same cannot be said for accomplishments of the mind or character however. You are not likely to be a great musician, artist, writer, or scholar, simply because one or even both of your parents were, or are. You could possibly be said to have an increased aptitude for learning, but this is by no means guaranteed. This is precisely the reason why we do not see many members of the same family becoming great scientists, or painters, or writers, etc. If these traits were passed down from mothers and fathers to their children, then the idea of the hereditary ruling principle could in some senses be valid. The argument would be that the father was a great political thinker and humanist, so it follows that the son would be also, and that would be reason enough for him being elevated to a position of power. However, as I have just pointed out, these types of traits are not passed on. It is well known that moral cretins and cowards can be born to men and women of extremely good character, and that sometimes all of the tutoring and education in the world cannot change this salient fact. In addition, tales of mad kings are ubiquitous throughout history, probably because of the fact that offspring from a small gene pool naturally have more defects, both mental and physical, than those that come from normal families. This is well understood and needs no further explanation from myself.

The objection to a heredity monarchy from a position of increasing reason and enlightenment should be obvious. At first glance it is simply absurd to rely on heredity as a guarantee of fitness to rule or a position of authority. This is why, in every other office of government, regular elections are commonplace, and hereditary dictatorships are shunned and despised. If you do not agree with my points thus far, then how would you feel about a hereditary doctor treating your children, or a hereditary maths teacher educating them? Or perhaps even a hereditary Prime Minister making decisions that you did not elect them to make? These propositions are ridiculous, yet many countries in the world put up with this attack on their intelligence and abuse of their tolerance. It becomes even more insufferable when you learn that there is no way to abolish this, and you have no say in whether the royal house stays or goes. I am of the mind that it should be abolished, and looked back upon with quaint fondness, much like you may look back upon a past relationship, which at the time was bearable, but which you realise after the fact was neither necessary nor useful.

At its heart, the hereditary principle is simply undemocratic. The right to vote and the right of the people to decide who should run their country and look after their interests has come about after many hundreds of years of strife and turmoil, and the fact that the head of state is someone who cannot be voted out, who cannot be appealed to, and who, when she dies, will pass on the crown to the most immediate member of her own family, negates all of the progress that we have supposedly made.

Amazingly, Prince Phillip has said that the hereditary ruling principle has served us, meaning the British people, well enough for many hundreds of years, so he sees no reason to change it now. I cannot think of a more arrogant claim. Would he have this opinion if he were on the other side of the fence, and it was someone he did not vote for being born to serve in the highest seat of office? I think not.

Related to the idea of heredity, at least traditionally, is the concept of class. Granted, our version is not as extreme as India's caste system for example, but nevertheless it does play a role in suppressing certain groups of people and elevating others. In this country, class and the class system have been a part of the mental furniture for as long as history has been written down. This is no surprise, as we as a species are tribal in nature, and naturally prefer the company of people who look like us, think like us, talk like us, and act like us. This is undoubtedly a flaw in the human condition, but I see no way of changing this anytime soon. It just so happens that the class system is this writ large, with certain areas of society propping themselves up and putting others down. It would perhaps be too easy to say that this divide can be bridged by the amassment of wealth, but this is not the case. There are plenty of people, in this country at least, who would consider David Beckham, a multimillionaire if ever there was one, as in a lower social class than themselves, even though he may earn many times what they currently do. It is of course possible to go up or down classes, if there is such a thing as a class ladder, but the ways of doing this are not that clear, at least at first glance. Speech definitely has something to do with it, as Orwell famously paraphrased Mr Wyndham Lewis, when he remarked that the English working class are branded on the tongue. It is more or less true today that you can tell someones background by the way they speak, and if you are good with accents, it is also possible to tell which part of the country they come from. This is also the case if you listen to what words people use for everyday objects; toilet, lavatory, and loo, for example. We were treated to an utterly pathetic show of this mentality when it was announced that Prince William had chosen for his bride the quite normal, if maybe middle to upper class, figure of Catherine Middleton. I was not the only one to notice snide remarks and comments that said not so plainly that maybe she wasn't *quite* socially mobile enough to be joining the royal family. It is easy to see why these and other cretinous remarks were made, as if anyone can marry into the royal family, and then in theory be placed on the throne, then the entire mystique surrounding it comes crashing down. The monarchy can only keep going if everyone, or a majority, believe, much like the story of Peter Pan, and once the cracks start to show, it may be too late to fix the damage that has been done. The conclusion is clear; if anyone can marry into the royal family, then their bloodline is not divine, and it is not anymore special than anyone else's. If they are not any different from you or I, then how do they claim the throne, especially if (as we saw in the earlier chapter concerning divine right) they claim no special right to rule?

If we must make one final objection to the hereditary principle it is that the royal family has not been the same from the very first king. You may think this does not seem too problematic, but surely the whole point of the hereditary principle is that it is everlasting, enduring, and unbroken! If the very first king was good enough biologically, then every member of his family, even up to the present day would be just as fit to rule. How is it possible to take the current monarchs claim seriously, that they are the only family allowed to rule and inherit the throne? This small example should expose the fact that the whole system of monarchy is not God made, but man made.

To summarise, the principle of heredity must be, and can only be, the ultimate point of objection to any monarchical system. All of the other objections can only be critiqued once the hereditary principle has been affirmed, as without it, there is no monarchy.

CHAPTER 5

The powers that are never used

> Experience hath shown, that even under the best forms of government those entrusted with power have, in time, and by slow operations, perverted it into tyranny.
>
> - Thomas Jefferson

It is understood, or at least affirmed by nearly all royalists, that the powers that the monarchy have are limited, and cannot be used as a serious objection. This chapter will aim to dispel this myth, and with it shine some light onto an aspect of the monarchy that is examined not nearly often enough.

One of the most common rebuttals to republicans like myself is that the powers that the monarch currently have are often said to be purely ceremonial, or that that the queen "reigns but she does not rule". Others will say that even though the monarch does have certain powers, they are never used, so what does it matter?

The exact and precise list of all royal prerogatives have never been revealed, which should arouse suspicion in even the slowest mind, but in 2004 some of the powers were published and made known. It is true that the powers that the monarch enjoys were severely limited and handicapped in the Glorious Revolution of 1688, as Article 1 of the Bill of Rights states that the "power of suspending the laws or the execution of laws by regal authority without consent of Parliament is illegal." The Bill also confirmed that Parliament had the right to limit the use of remaining prerogatives, which required the monarch to dismiss and call Parliament at certain times. To begin with, we must look at the powers that are given to the monarch, or that they affirm they have, in order to understand exactly what impact they have on the lives of ordinary people. There are still many powers that the monarch not only can, but does use, and these are as follows:

Domestic and foreign powers
1. The power to dismiss and appoint a Prime Minister
2. The power to dismiss and appoint other ministers
3. The power to summon and prorogue Parliament
4. The power to grant or refuse Royal Assent to bills
5. The power to commission officers in the Armed Forces
6. The power to command the Armed Forces
7. The power to issue and withdraw passports
8. The power to grant Prerogative of mercy
9. The power to grant honours
10. The power to create corporations by Royal Charter
11. The power to appoint bishops in the Church of England
12. The power to ratify and make treaties
13. The power to declare War and Peace
14. The power to deploy the Armed Forces overseas
15. The power to recognise states
16. The power to credit and receive diplomats

Let me be clear; this is not an exhaustive list by any means, as I have already explained, and my critique now requires that we examine some of these powers to discern exactly what it allows the monarch to do or not do.

The power to appoint and dismiss a Prime Minister is theoretically governed by Royal Prerogative. The monarch is able to technically appoint whomever he or she likes as Prime Minister, but usually this is the person who commands a majority in the House of Commons. This is all well and good, but there are far too many technicalities for my liking, and many other peoples too. Today, the monarch exercises the prerogative almost exclusively in line with the advice of her government. Leyland noted that:

> *"The present Queen is kept very closely in touch with the exercise of governmental power by means of a weekly audience with the prime minister during which she is fully briefed about the affairs of government ... But it should be emphasised that the prime minister is not under any obligation to take account of royal opinions."*

Why, if the Prime Minister is not under any obligation to take on the monarchs opinions, does he have to sit through weekly meetings with the said monarch? If the exercise serves no purpose, then why is it still part of our governmental process? The monarch is also said to have the "right to be consulted, the right to encourage, and the right to warn". The point here is that the queen or whomever the monarch is at the time, has the right to be consulted and informed of the governments goings on before and as they happen. Do I, as a tax paying citizen, have this right? Why should an unelected and hereditary head of state be privy to all manner of issues of national security, when that person has not been elected into the position by the very people that elected the ministers in government?

There is another excuse trotted out here, that says that as the Prime Minister of the day has to meet with the queen on a weekly basis, and in effect that he or she has someone higher to answer to, that this keeps him honest. This is accepted by some as a well reasoned argument, unaware of the yawning trapdoor right under their feet. The question that should spring to mind is this; who is the *queen* answerable to? In the early days of society it may have been plausibly believed that, divinely appointed as monarchs were, they were answerable only to the creator, but now that this belief has faded (or so we are told) then who does the queen turn to to keep her own views congruent and in line with what is in the peoples best interests?

In addition, as I will mention in other parts of this book, Elizabeth II is a completely different person than Prince Charles. Are we to believe, that a man like him who has shown that he has strong opinions even on trivial matters like architecture, will *not* be influenced by those opinions when he inevitably has to appoint a Prime Minister?

The queen or whomever is the current monarch also has the power to appoint and dismiss other governmental ministers, a power that no other person has. In practice, and via tradition, this is normally carried out by other ministers on the queens behalf, but the point remains that the ultimate power resides with the monarch. There is not much more to say here other than it is quite obviously not a correct or moral way to run a governmental system, and is open to all sorts of abuses by definition. Again, I need only mention the name of Charles here to demonstrate how, even if this power does not pose a problem at this moment in time, that it will when he becomes king. The action of appointing Prime Minister is carried out rarely, whereas the action of appointing other ministers may be a regular occurrence. Again, are we really to believe that a person who is quick to judge and who makes up his mind on things without ever considering the evidence or following logic to its conclusion, will be able to make impartial and intelligent judgements?

The power to prorogue, that is to suspend parliament without actually dissolving it, still lies with the monarch, although this is normally only done with the consent or under the request of the Prime Minister. Again, there are far too many technicalities here for my liking. If the process is simply a ceremonial one, them why not remove all of the "technical" power from the monarch and put it in the hands of the people that we have elected to represent us. Royalists will also point to the fact that the power to dissolve parliament was abrogated by the Fixed-term Parliaments Act 2011, but section 6(1) of the Act specifically states that the monarchs power to prorogue parliament is not affected by the Act, so this is simply a moot point.

The power to grant or refuse Royal Assent simply means that the queen has the right and responsibility to make bills into law. In theory the queen, and any future monarch, could decide to refuse assent. Royalists will rise to the defence of the monarchy at this point, saying that the last time that royal assent was refused was during the reign of Queen Anne. Even though the right to refuse assent has faded from use, George V believed at the time that he could veto the Third Irish Home Rule Bill. Jennings commented that "it was assumed by the King throughout that he had not only the legal power but the constitutional right to refuse assent." So, as we can see, even as recently as one hundred years ago, monarchs were a power unto themselves. The simple fact, that cannot be denied, is that the right still remains, so what is to say that a future monarch, or the current one, will refuse assent to a bill that the people wish to be passed into law?

The most damning, but not perhaps the most well known example of this ability to either say yay or nay to bills becoming law, was documented by the founding fathers of the United States, in the Declaration of Independence of 1776.

I examine this landmark piece of writing later on in *Part III*, but it is enough to say here that the king was not innocent when it came to the fact of giving Royal Assent to bills that the people living on another continent thought were in their best interests.

The power to commission officers in the Armed Forces is a pretty uncontroversial point on its face, but under further examination this is not really the case. It is well known that only certain types, or perhaps we should say classes, of people ever really become officers in the military system in this country. There are of course numerous exceptions, but can anyone reading this say that there are not more Edward's or Charlie's with the title of officer in the armed forces than there are Steve's or Frank's? I saw this happen in miniature, albeit in a completely different discipline, when I was a young man playing rugby. I was lucky enough to play at quite a high level for a number of years, representing my county and other district teams. At the time many people were overlooked for positions, not for any other reason than the colour of their school tie. This school tie selection was rampant, and was made worse by the fact that at that age parents were often heavily involved, as after all, they had to drive the youngsters to the games, they wanted their child to get ahead, and they would pull whatever strings they could to get a position for their own offspring. This is understandable, and I daresay if there is ever a point in my life where I can do something to open doors for my children, then I will do it without hesitation. Now, this is not so much of a problem when we are talking about who does or does not get into a trivial sports team, but surely this does have an effect if it is present in our military system, where ability and merit are far more important than bloodline, or how you speak, or whereabouts in the country you were raised.

The power to command the Armed Forces is a given for the monarch, as they normally inherit the title of Head of State, Head of the Church, and Head of the Armed Forces. Many people will point to the fact that having a non politician in charge of the forces stops the military coming under the control of a single person, or a treasonous politician, but a moments thought reveals this to be fatuous. If an army can be swayed to follow a particularly unwholesome politician or general, then surely they would be more than capable of following the orders of an unwholesome monarch. It has also been contemptuously said that unlike North American military personnel, who swear their allegiance to the constitution, our brave men and women swear their oath to a person, which in this moment in time is the queen. I would have thought that swearing upon a set of principles, regardless of if they are only written on a piece of paper, is a much more noble and sensible thing to do, rather than a moderate form of idol worship, which swearing allegiance to the queen actually is.

It is my opinion, and I would think many other peoples as well, that the head of the armed forces should be the highest ranked individual at that particular time. Surely only by going through the ranks does a person have an idea of what it is like to be a member of the military, and would therefore be much less likely to make rash decisions, for good or ill. Even if this is an unworkable and unsafe idea, surely we must be able to come up with a better method of picking the head of the armed forces than by heredity?

As an aside, there is something that has always angered me about the royal family, in the obscene amount of medals the males wear on their ceremonial dress. Can any of them really say, apart from Prince Harry and a couple of other individuals, who it must be admitted have seen military action, that they have earned those medals? How they have the audacity to show their faces in public, and dress like that in front of other much longer serving but lower ranked members of the armed forces, is beyond my comprehension.

The power to appoint bishops and archbishops is not that controversial in and of itself, especially after you consider that the monarch is the head of the church, but here again we have the fact that the figure is a human being. Human beings have their own agendas, regardless of how much we might like to think to the contrary, and there has never been and will never be a person born who is completely impartial. It is not hard to imagine what will happen if we do end up with Charles III. The prince has already said that he wishes to be Defender of Faith, and it would not be unthinkable that he might appoint more fundamentalist clergymen than his mother evidently has. Many people will see this is as a lot of worrying over nothing, but we only have to look to any society that starts to lean more towards fundamentalism to see what happens, and the outcome is never good. It also begs the question; what qualities does the monarch possess that others do not, that enables them and them alone to be eligible to appoint these holy men?

Now you may say, and many people do, that the monarch does not use the powers that I have briefly outlined. Even if this were the case, and I have proven that it is not, then why are the powers granted at all? Would they be used in the event of an emergency? What sort of emergency would they be used in, if any? If the head of state is a purely ceremonial position, a talking point that is regularly recited by royalists, then why are the powers granted to the head of state? These questions and others need answering, not by spokespersons of the royal house, but by the members of the royal house themselves.

Even if the current monarch does not and never did use these powers, which is not the case, there will be a moment in the not too distant future when Prince Charles will become King. If you haven't realised it yet, Prince Charles and Queen Elizabeth II are not the same person. They have different agendas, different politics, different temperaments, and differing views on what they think the monarchy should stand for. Of course, Charles could take the throne and go about his business in much the same way as his mother has done, but he could also become a very political king, a situation that would become utterly insufferable.

Speaking of Prince Charles, it has become clear that the belief that the monarchy does not and cannot influence policy is simply false. There are numerous examples but perhaps the best, and the most enlightening, especially considering that we will soon no doubt be saddled with King Charles III, is the furore over the "Black spider memos", so called for Prince Charles' distinctive black ink scrawl which are contained in letters directed to minsters in various positions of government. There are two main points of interest, or perhaps more specifically concern, here. The first is that the letters were written at all. The monarchs are meant to be impartial, and are said to have the right to advise, warn, and consult, not to lobby. The second is that the Freedom of Information request to see the content of these letters and memos, filed repeatedly by the Guardian newspaper, has been denied thus far. Perhaps most worryingly of all, the attorney general actually blocked the release of some of the black spider memos after a Freedom of Information request by the Guardian newspaper. Dominic Grieve stopped the release of "particularly frank" letters from Charles to ministers, saying that their disclosure would "potentially have undermined his position of political neutrality", "damage the Prince of Wales's ability to perform his duties when he becomes king" and "would be seriously damaging to his role as a future monarch". For the attorney general not to release the letters into the public sphere can mean only one thing; that the letters contain evidence of Prince Charles directly trying to interfere and influence ministers on matters of public policy, yet we are routinely told by the supporters of the monarchy that their powers are limited and that they do not get involved in politics.

The fact that Price Charles has intervened in government affairs and has written letters and memos directly to ministers should not be news to anyone, especially after learning that Charles thinks of himself as a "meddling prince". The letters and memos themselves have been reported as covering a wide range of topics - which is surely worse - from environment, to architecture, to genetically modified foods, to work and pensions, and children's education. It is not known, at least as of yet, whether Charles was successful in his lobbying attempts in all of his endeavours, but we can take a look at one example to see that in some cases he did apparently get his own way. In 2009 he wrote to the Qatari royal family, who at the time were the developers of the Chelsea Barracks site in west London. The architect on that project was Richard Rogers, whose design Charles labelled "unsuitable", and "a gigantic experiment with the very soul of our capital city". Now, I am not saying that the prince was successful in his critique of the architects work, but the fact is that Richard Rogers was subsequently removed, and the Prince's own Foundation for the Built Environment tasked with finding an alternative design. Rogers later commented that the Prince had also intervened to block his designs of the Royal Opera House and the Paternoster Square, and called the prince's actions "an abuse of power", and "unconstitutional". If you thought that this unwelcome intervention went unnoticed by the media or uncriticised you would be wrong. Mr Justice Vos remarked that the attention of the Prince was "unexpected and unwelcome", but funnily enough, many people both in the public sphere and the establishment were disappointed with the judges remarks. Perhaps they would prefer a man with no architectural experience to choose which multimillion pound projects go ahead or not. Graham Smith, campaign manager for Republic, a lobby group which calls for the abolition of the monarchy, said the case raised wider questions about Charles. He said:

> "It is quite clear that the Prince is using his position to sway matters of public policy by approaching parties outside the democratic process. How many other government decisions are being influenced by the Prince's behind-closed-doors lobbying?"

Moving to someone who actually does know a thing or two about architecture, Ruth Reed, the president of the Royal Institute of British Architects, said:

"The Prince of Wales is entitled to raise concerns about architecture but we regret that on this occasion he failed to engage with the planning process entirely openly and appropriately. One person in a position of considerable influence in public life should not be able to exert undue influence on democratic decision making."

Now that we know about this single instance of royal meddling where it was not wanted, there remains only one question to ask; if Charles is prepared to get deeply involved with a seemingly unimportant issue such as architecture when he is *not* king, what will his behaviour be like once he has even more unchecked power at his disposal? To shine even more light onto this subject, I reproduce below a list of examples of Charles having interfered with public policy and in the public sphere. The information is taken from the website of the campaign group Republic:

In 1984 Charles described a scheme by architect Peter Ahrends for an extension to the National Gallery as a "monstrous carbuncle on the face of a much-loved and elegant friend". The scheme was subsequently scrapped and it took Ahrends many years to recover his reputation.

Charles's views on education were made clear during an employment tribunal in 2004, when his handwritten memo was used as evidence. "What is wrong with people nowadays? Why do they all seem to think they are qualified to do things far above their capabilities?" he asked. "This is all to do with the learning culture in schools. It is a consequence of a child-centred education system which tells people they can become pop stars, high court judges or brilliant TV presenters or infinitely more competent heads of state without ever putting in the necessary work or having the natural ability."

In 2006 Charles used a speech at the World Health Assembly in Geneva to call on governments to fund complementary medicines such as homeopathy – at a time when the issues was the subject of intense political and professional debate.

In 2007 Charles personally lobbied the Medicines and Healthcare products Regulatory Agency (MHRA) to include complementary and alternative medicines within its remit, despite opposition from scientists. Shortly after, the MHRA relaxed its rules of herbal medicines.

Charles successfully lobbied the Qatari royal family to ditch plans for a £3 billion block of flats on the Chelsea Barracks site because he disliked the modernist design. The Prince's Foundation for the Built Environment, Charles's architecture lobby group, was reported to the charity commission for its role in the dispute.

In April 2009 Republic reported the Prince's Foundation for the Built Environment to the charity commission, accusing the charity of acting as Charles's "private lobbying firm".

In October 2009 Charles met with Andy Burnham, then health secretary, at Clarence House to lobby for complementary and alternative medicines to be available on the NHS. The pair met at Clarence House.

In his memoirs, published in 2010, Peter Mandelson recounts that Tony Blair asked him to tell Charles to stop his "unhelpful" and "irresponsible" attempts to influence government policy.

In March 2010 Republic reported the Prince's Foundation for Integrated Health to the charity commission, accusing the foundation's staff of pursuing a public vendetta against Edzard Ernst, a professor of complementary medicine.

Charles and his education group successfully lobbied education secretary Michael Gove on the new national curriculum.

Papers disclosed in 2011 under freedom of information rules revealed that Charles's charities had asked the government to change policies on a number of politically sensitive topics.

In 2012 an investigation by Republic revealed that aides from Charles's charities enjoy privileged access to politicians and civil servants. His organisations held at least 18 face-to-face meetings with senior cabinet ministers and top Downing Street officials over a two year period.

Draft NHS guidance warning that there is no evidence that homeopathy works was suppressed following lobbying by the Foundation for Integrated Health, Charles's alternative medicine charity.

January 2013 Charles attacked the British education system, complaining that schools fail to teach "life skills" and "character".

Although we have touched on Freedom of Information already, it is worthwhile examining this area in a little more detail. The Freedom of Information Act 2000, is an Act of Parliament that creates a public right of access to information held by public authorities. The full provisions of the Act came into effect on the 1st January 2005, and were brought about for the simple reason of making public bodies and organisations more accountable, by allowing any member of the public or journalistic sphere to request to know answers to any questions that they may have about the organisation in question. Through this Act there are a number of things that have been discovered about the behaviours of the royal family themselves, and some of the more damaging examples follow next:

In 2004 the Queen asked ministers for a poverty handout to help heat her palaces but was rebuffed because they feared it would be a public relations disaster. Royal aides were told that the £60m worth of energy-saving grants were aimed at families on low incomes and if the money was given to Buckingham Palace instead of housing associations or hospitals it could lead to "adverse publicity" for the Queen and the government.

A "financial memorandum" formalising the relationship between the sovereign and ministers set out tough terms on how the Queen can spend the £38.2m handed over by Parliament each year to pay for her staff and occupied palaces.

The Queen requested more public money to pay for the upkeep of her crumbling palaces while allowing minor royals and courtiers to live in rent-free accommodation.

As early as 2004 Sir Alan Reid, the Keeper of the Privy Purse, had unsuccessfully put the case to the Department for Culture, Media and Sport for a substantial increase in the £15m-a-year grant to maintain royal buildings.

A letter exchange revealed a tussle over who has control of £2.5m gained from the sale of Kensington Palace land. Ministers said it belonged to the state, while Buckingham Palace said it belonged to the Queen.

To show why the Freedom of Information Act should be applied to all public bodies, including the monarchy, we only have to look at an example given by Ian Davidson, a former member of the Parliament's Public Accounts Committee (PAC). Mr Davidson told The Independent newspaper that:

"I'm astonished that the government should find time to seek to cover up royal finances. When I was on the PAC what we wanted was more disclosure not less. Every time we examined royal finances we found extravagance and indulgence as well as abuse of expenses by junior royals. Everywhere we looked, there were savings to be made for the Government. This sends the wrong message about public disclosure and accountability."

I don't know about you, but the finances of a public institution that is directly paid for by the taxpayer, and furthermore, whose members are not picked by the people but by heredity, should be as open to critique and examination as possible. Paul Flynn, another member of the Public Accounts Committee, described the special protection for the Royals as "indefensible". Mr Flynn was more right than he knew. It absolutely is indefensible, and just goes to show how powerless most of us are if we wish to know more about our unelected head of state and their extended family.

In my personal opinion there is only a single reason why the monarchy would want themselves to be exempt from Freedom of Information requests, and this is to limit the amount that the public knows or can know about their inner workings. This would no doubt answer the question of whether they are using more power then their supporters say they are using, and would expose any powers that they do have access to and put them under greater scrutiny. In addition, as I have said previously, the whole facade of the monarchic system is kept going by the fact that the population at large consider it to be mysterious and ethereal, and in my mind, to expose the magic behind it would lead to the inevitable downfall of the monarchy itself. It is quite clear that it cannot exist, in its current state anyway, if the people no longer see the royals as something more than themselves.

To conclude this chapter, it is clear that the argument that the monarchy does not have many powers, let alone use them, is utterly false. The monarchy does enjoy wide reaching powers, and the monarchy does use them as they see fit, even if it is under the pretence of tradition and convention. The acquisition of power, and the right to use it, should not be awarded by the principle of heredity, but on the merits of the individual. It is clear to me, and should be to any thinking person, that a truly democratic society cannot exist unless these powers are relinquished.

CHAPTER 6

Effects on the people

The natural cause of the human mind is certainly
from credulity to skepticism.

- Thomas Jefferson

One aspect of having a monarchy that is either left
out of the argument completely, or is acknowledged
but then not followed up on, is the effect that being
deferent to a group or family of people has on
society. Serfdom and the unquestioning allegiance
of the populace would have been extremely useful
in the early days of kingship. Education would have
been almost non-existent, except amongst the
nobility, and literacy rates would have been
shockingly low. In addition, religious fervour and
belief would have been almost utter and complete.
Now imagine that you are an ambitious and driven
man, that wants to rule over these people. It would
not take such a person long to come up with the
idea that says that the God people believe in, at that

point the Christian God, has put you in power over them, and to reject this is to commit blasphemy of the highest degree.

I am not the first person to note that the want or need to have a permanent loving parent, or big brother, is more or less ubiquitous throughout all human groups, and I think that this is true for obvious reasons. Who wouldn't like to think that there is someone out there, looking after you, caring about you, caring what happens to your children, and who is a solid, immovable figure, who remains steadfast whilst all around is changing. The fact that Queen Elisabeth II has been in power for more than sixty years resonates with many people that I have spoken to, and is sometimes one of the main reasons that they still support the monarchy. The job of a parent however is to eventually make room, and to get out of the way. It is not healthy to have, and not healthy to wish for, an all powerful, supervising parent, and it does nothing but infantilise the mentality of those people who are the subjects of its affection.

In more recent years, the obsession with other peoples lives has grown to a very large degree, with the rise of specialist websites and television channels devoted to nothing but the adoration of mediocre human beings. What with the advent of the internet, widely distributed magazines, and all other manner of image based media, it is now easier than it has ever been to read about that celebrity wedding, or that stars divorce, or any other scandal that you care to think of. That people vicariously live other peoples lives should not be news to anyone, and it can at least be understood that many people wish to escape the day to day mundaneness of what they consider their own lives to be, but this practice must in the end be harmful, both to their own mental faculties, and of the social mobility of society as a whole.

The mentality of the serf, or of the slave, is dangerous not just on its face, but also because they are then susceptible to perform all sorts of atrocities because of their own serfdom. Those poor souls in North Korea would undoubtedly carry out whatever heinous acts that their leaders would order them to, because of the history of inculcation that has permeated that hermetic state. Whatever we might think of a place like North Korea, what it suffers from is not too much critical thinking or too much scepticism. If the populace did suffer from those things, then a place like North Korea would not exist in the first place. Now of course, I am not comparing Kim-Il Sung and his offspring to the royal family, but the similar ways that the people look up to the two dynasties is too glaring to omit. In both cases, uninformed people are recruited en masse to not say anything derogatory about the leaders, to not question their aims, objectives, and methods in governing, and to bend the knee whenever it is required of them. The punishments in each situation are worlds apart however. In North Korea, if you have the bravery to dissent, it is often at the expense of not just your own life, but that of the next three generations of your immediate family. Rightly the political labour prisons like Camp 22 are regarded with unquenchable fear by the vast majority of North Koreans.

In this country, there were some people in my immediate circle of family and friends who were trying to persuade me to publish this book under a pen name. I have done this, but not for the reasons that they expressed, and instead so that the argument would be the most important part of this pamphlet, and not the identity of the author. Now of course, it would be very unlikely that someone would make a death threat or other action against me simply for writing and expressing my own opinions on an important subject, but then I am sure that Salman Rushdie did not expect that he would have to go into hiding for over ten years for the "crime" of writing a work of fiction. As has been said by people more intelligent than myself, the consequence of those who censor is that they make themselves prisoners of their own opinions, and then lack the means of changing them. The ability to criticise anything, no matter how sacred, and to not be persecuted for doing so, is how progress in made. It is a simple fact that the deference paid to the monarchs and the hereditary principle in general is an inculcator of tolerance, which is not a good thing in this aspect. Tolerance for ideas is fine, but there must at least be the potential to criticise, but the barrier to criticism that results from the constant looking up of lower classes to higher ones does not do us any favours. This leads us directly into censorship, and the suppression of ideas and viewpoints that may be offensive to some. Though most people would profess that the censored draw the short straw, it may surprise you to know that the real damage done is to the censors themselves. By banning certain media, the censors prohibit themselves from the means and methods of changing their own opinions. These actions are often done in the name of public decency, or in the name of protecting some minority or other from harm, but simply does nothing but anger the censored. Amazingly, until 1968, an official called the Lord Chamberlain held the power to censor plays and productions taking place in British theatres, especially if the reigning monarchs were depicted. The situation was even stranger, as previous monarchs were allowed to be represented, but only if they were at least three generations in the past. Again, these are absurd and quite clearly man made laws, constructed to appease a divinely appointed man or woman, to which criticism is to at least have been expected.

The biggest problem in realising that mass opinion can be so powerful, is the question of what can be done to change it when reason and logic dictate that it must be changed? If the mob consistently votes against their own interests, then there is very little that can be done realistically. Peoples thought processes and opinions cannot be changed by force, and perhaps the only method of seeing change in this area is by education. Education of the young, and the ability of them to think critically may well be the only safeguard against hysteria, mass stupidity, and other mindsets that are harmful to society as a whole. Perhaps the most extreme example we could examine would be that of North Korea, a state that I have already mentioned. Is it to be believed, that if the population of that country were exposed to the methods of critical thinking and scepticism, that they would not rise up and overthrow the tyrannical regime that has them in their grip? The very reason that North Korea is so dangerous is because it mainly consists of millions upon millions of stunted men, women, and children, both in body and mind, that accept almost everything they are told with unquestioning fealty. Our society is light years away from that one, but only in some respects. If the voice of criticism is suppressed by the very people whose job it is to critique, then the population as a whole have little chance of changing their own minds, let alone having the means to change them themselves.

To summarise, the serf mentality is congruent with an uneducated and ignorant populace, a situation that will nearly always result in the people voting against their best interests. This is not just harmful, but cannot be allowed to propagate if we are ever going to outgrow the monarchy. The two concepts, that of a hereditary ruler and an informed electorate can never co exist because the electorate, by being educated, simply would not permit a system such as monarchy to exist. It is my opinion that this state of affairs be not just desirable, but essential.

CHAPTER 7

Unworthy successors

> When we are planning for posterity, we ought to
> remember that virtue is not hereditary.
> > - Thomas Paine

If you disagreed completely with my points made
in the earlier chapter entitled *The problem with
heredity*, then this chapter will certainly convince
you that picking heads of state by virtue of their
bloodline is a moronic and idiotic thing to do.
There will come a day when the current monarch
dies, and as the laws and traditions of heredity
stipulate, as soon as that happens her son Charles
Windsor, the Prince of Wales, will immediately
become the head of the state, the head of the
church, and the head of the armed forces. This may
seem like an important position for a single man to
have, so you might think that rigorous training is
undergone by all members of the royal family to

best prepare them for the eventuality that they may come into the throne. It is no surprise to hear that no such training is undertaken, and again, seemingly the only qualification needed is for you to be able to call the current monarch mother or father. This is a laughable situation to find ourselves in, especially if we dig a little deeper into exactly what the man touted to be our next king thinks and says in public, not to mention what he thinks and says in private.

Prince Charles is in a very strange position, and perhaps a unique one amongst all people who live in this small country we call home, for he cannot start the job he was born for until his mother dies. I cannot imagine what this feels like, and really would not like to, but how can this sort of situation be healthy for the mind?

Charles' early life was one of privilege, with huge sums of money being spent on his education, only for him to come out of schooling with a B and a C in his A levels. This achievement, ordinarily, would not be enough to make it to the prestigious halls of Oxford or Cambridge, but being the son of the Queen, small things like merit are not required. So, he was admitted to Cambridge, where he worked diligently and came out with a 2:2. You may scoff at my university result, of which I will not inform you, other than to say that it was certainly less than a 2:2, but I am not in line to be head of state, and would reject the post if it were offered to me. After his dazzling educational adventure, the young prince was enrolled into the Navy, where again he failed dismally. His exact antics here are not really important, but I think it is safe to say that he would not have started life at the bottom of the career ladder.

In his adult life, Charles has done no better. David Dimbleby, something of Charles' personal biographer, has written that that his staff "were uncomfortable with his tendency to reach instant conclusions on the basis of insufficient thought". Is this the type of person who we want as head of the armed forces, head of the church, and head of the state? I for one do not find this admission surprising, as it is quite clear that Prince Charles has contempt for reason, disdain for the scientific method, and considers the advances that we have made as a species with technology to be of little worth, except when flying in a jet to whatever function he is needed, perhaps I should say inflicted, upon.

There are many other things that the prince has said that require examination, many of them foolish and all them showing that he is not fit for the position into which he has been waiting for all of these years. About Galileo, that true genius that opened our eyes to the wonders of the cosmos and taught us our real place in the universe, he had the following to say:

> "This imbalance, where mechanistic thinking is so predominant, goes back at least to Galileo's assertion that there is nothing in Nature but quantity and motion. This is the view that continues to frame the general perception of the way the world works and how we fit within the scheme of things. As a result, Nature has been completely objectified – "She" has become an "it" – and we are persuaded to concentrate on the material aspect of reality that fits within Galileo's scheme."

I hate to break it to Prince Charles, but Galileo was right. Nature is nothing but quantity and motion, and the more we learn about the universe the truer this becomes. Far from sucking the life and soul out of the natural world however, I am of the firm belief that it makes it infinitely more beautiful. How would we have ever seen, for example, the mind altering pictures sent back from the Hubble Space telescope without the advances of science?

In other anti-science rants he has professed an interest in and been an advocate for homeopathic and other alternative medicine, that which all of the scientific evidence discredits, and has also insisted that the government fund alternative treatment centres, which they do.

In the realm of religion, Prince Charles has made it quite plain what he thinks of the millions of people in this country who do not have faith of any kind. He purports, as I explain in an earlier chapter, that he wants to be not just *Defender of the Faith* (as if prefacing faith with "the" makes it clear that we are talking about the Anglican religion), but defender of all faiths. On the face of it this seems like a nice, inclusive, progressive statement, and what could possibly be wrong with that? Many things as it turns out, the foremost one being that many millions of people have no faith, and are quite content to live their lives as if the supernatural dimension (for which no one has ever produced anything like convincing evidence) does not exist. I do not trust anybody completely that has faith of this kind, as they are basically admitting that they will believe anything on the grounds of little to no evidence at all. This is not too much of a problem if you keep it to yourself, and you are not able or willing to inflict your views on others around you, but here is a man that will be elevated to the highest position of power, on the grounds of nothing more than his bloodline, where he will get the chance to legislate and to promote his views to the very people that the public have elected to represent them. He has also exhibited an alarming tolerance of Islam, the so called religion of peace. I will say it now and I will say it plain; Islam is not a religion of peace. There may be certain verses in the Qur'an that could be said to be moral, but they are undone by many others. Let us take the simple fact of changing your religion or leaving Islam. You may think that it is entirely up to the individual what they believe, but Islam does not agree. The Hadith, or the doings and sayings of the prophet, explicitly states that an apostate, someone who leaves or changes their religion, must be killed. It does not say that they might be killed, or that they will only be killed in certain circumstances; it says that they must be killed, and the pretext for this is leaving or changing their religion. Now you may say that this law or command is not followed anymore, or at least it is not followed by any moderate muslim, but that would be missing the point completely. If this law or rule is not followed now, then it is because the progress of secular society and morality has shown it to be fatuous. For the average person on the street to support the ideals that this religion espouses is bad enough, but for the future head of state to do so is just plain idiotic, and shows a complete lack of respect for the ideals that produce a successful society, namely education, respect for and equality of women and minorities, separation of church and state, freedom of speech, and free inquiry and the ability to criticise anything, no matter how sacred the subject.

To show how dangerous the withered mind of Prince Charles is, and to show how he is not fit to become head of state, I refer you to the contents of a letter that he wrote in 2003, which was as follows:

> What is wrong with everyone nowadays? Why do they all seem to think they are qualified to do things far beyond their natural capabilities?
>
> This is all to do with the learning culture in schools. It is a consequence of the child-centred education. It tells people that they can be pop stars, high court judges or brilliant TV presenters or even infinitely more competent heads of state without ever putting in the necessary work, effort or having natural ability.
>
> It is the result of social utopianism which believes humanity can be genetically re-engineered to contradict the lessons of history and realities of nature.

The belief, by our potential, unelected, future head of state, that education should not be child centred because it gives them ideas above their station, is almost too disgusting to bother rebutting. Has Prince Charles followed his reasoning to its logical conclusion? If ever there were someone born that has none of the natural talent for the job they were born to do, it is him. I will say it simply and plainly; education, and the ability to be educated, are perhaps the only things that distinguish us from other forms of life. We are the only organism on the planet, as far as we know, that can reason, and for a man in Prince Charles' position to say that we should suppress this ability shows how utterly incompetent he is to do literally anything worthwhile, let alone become head of the state, head of the church, and head of the armed forces. For far too long has this man been fawned upon by nearly any reporter or journalist that will listen to his rantings, but the time for that is over.

Recently, it has become clear to anybody, even the most ardent royalist, that having a Charles III cannot be allowed to happen. David Dimbleby, again writing about the Prince, has said that he wishes to be a political king, and that he will rule over us with his knowledge and contacts and unique ability. I have news for the prince; this unwavering self confidence is the result of a lifetime of flattery, none of it deserved, and has so left him with the belief that he really does know what he is doing. In my opinion, and that of many others, nothing could be further from the truth.

If you have read thus far and simply believe that I am making a personal attack on the prince, you are mistaken. I am not making, and would never make an ad hominem attack on a current or future monarch, not out of respect or admiration, but simply because the persona of the current monarch at the time of writing is not my reason for abolishment of the monarchy, as I hope I have made plain. Still, the head of state is a person and as such their persona needs to be examined with a critical eye. It is all well and good to say that the queen has been exemplary in her rule, or reign, but the hereditary principle, by definition, ensures that sooner or later we will be saddled with an ignoramus, an imbecile, or someone who is downright dangerous, as I hope I have shown in the case of Prince Charles.

Whilst there is no doubt that the more senior members of the royal family are fair game for criticism, it may seem in poor taste to target the younger members, but this objection must not be permitted. Shifting our gaze to the potential future king, Prince William, there is no doubt that this apparently well mannered and caring young man, along with his younger brother Prince Harry, was dealt a harsh and cruel blow on the death of his mother. He quite understandably, but wrongly, blamed the paparazzi for her death, and one can see why he would do that. It does not change the fact that the man responsible for his mothers death was the driver (no matter how much he believed, and everyone else it seemed, that the photographers were responsible, especially in the immediate aftermath of the accident). Prince William has also expressed anger at the British and world press for what he sees as intrusion into his private life, but what did he expect? First of all, his mother was a voluntary member of a controversial ruling dynasty that the public pays for, and as such, they surely deserve some scrutiny. His mother did not have to join into that family. She could have quite easily not become an HRH, and avoided all of the media fuss that comes from being part of the monarchy. It is also worth noting that though Prince William may feel like he is stuck in the charade, he can quite easily leave, simply by renouncing his titles and renouncing his right to the throne. He is completely free to do this, and I would support his right to live a free and prosperous life if he did so, but until that time, he must expect to come under the media spotlight. It is not my interest that he must suffer from, as I do not wish to see pictures of the royal family, or any celebrity for that matter, as that sort of thing does not and probably will not ever interest me. However, there are many millions of people in this country and around the world that are very interested in the goings on of the royals, so until the time comes when they are not, the monarch and the monarchs in waiting will have to get used to the attention of the media. For William, it may comfort him, or horrify him, I am not sure which, to know that recent polls have shown that a great majority of the people in this country would prefer him to take the throne in place of his father. I am sure that he would be a better king than Prince Charles, but many people seem to be missing the point, which is that the public does not get to pick who becomes the next monarch. If you do wish to pick the next head of state, then start calling for a republic.

If you read the previous chapter concerning the problem with heredity, and did not find it a convincing argument, I hope that now you can see how there is no guarantee that whomever escapes the royal womb is automatically the best person for the job. There is of course a good chance that a man or woman with real moral courage and great intellect may be born to a member of the royal family, but unfortunately, there is also an equal chance of us ending up with a scientifically illiterate, politically interfering, alternative medicine supporting, pseudo intellectual.

CHAPTER 8

The Diana episode

"Back then: to be paid more, one needed to increase the number of things that are by him known. Today: to be paid more, one needs to increase the number of people by whom he is known."

- Mokokoma Mokhonoana

In the last chapter of this section we are going to look at an event that for all intents and purposes was a non-event. I am talking about the short life and death of Diana Spencer. The early life of Diana Spencer was a privileged one, of that there is no doubt. She was born to one of the most aristocratic families that survive in Britain, and was almost destined to either marry into or become part of whatever the ruling dynasty was at the time. Her father was John Spencer, Viscount Althorp, and her mother was the Honourable Frances Roche, who in turn was the daughter of the 4th Baron Fermoy. Diana became Lady Diana Spencer when her father inherited the title of Earl Spencer in 1975. It may confuse you as to why I am bringing all of this up, but I have a very good reason. The reason is that Diana Spencer was someone who's actions were judged by her reputation, and not the other way around. This is no fault of her own necessarily, but more the fault of the journalistic profession, whose job, indeed mandate it is, to ask questions and challenge the status quo.

We can get a glimpse of the type of person that Diana Spencer was, and how, even for all of her apparent sympathy with those less fortunate, thought herself above the rest of us, when we recall an exchange that apparently took place a year before her divorce. According to Tina Brown, Prince Phillip had remarked, "If you don't behave my girl, we'll take your title away". This is bad enough in and of itself, as if the prince thinks that he has the right to award and take away imaginary - to me anyway - titles of merit. Diana Spencer apparently retorted that "my title (The Lady Diana Frances Spencer) is a lot older than yours, Phillip". This goes way beyond simple arrogance. Who could have possibly sat there and thought that was a fit way for one human mammal to talk to another? Did Diana Spencer really think that her invented title made her more moral, more intellectual, more ethical, or more qualified to rule over the rest of us, than the man she was speaking to? Again, the absurdity of the hereditary principle rears its ugly head. Diana Spencer was simply born into a family that happened to award her a title, and the worst of it was that she was never required to prove that it was hers to have, or that she deserved it in the first place. Again, we see the automatic assumption that some mammals are due a certain level of respect, and get so used to never hearing a bad word said to them, much like Prince Charles, that when their actions or motives *are* questioned it is met with gasps and shocked faces.

Many people, even republicans, claimed to have been shocked and saddened by the death of Diana Spencer, but I was not one of them. I remember where I was when the news came on the television to announce that Diana, then *not* an HRH as almost everyone seems to forget, had died in a tunnel on the grimy streets of Paris. I was in my parents living room, being about fourteen years of age at the time. The television was on, and we watched as all manner of frauds and mountebanks streamed by one by one offering their condolences. I said at the time something along the lines of "I don't see what the big deal is?", to which my father replied, "two young boys have just lost their mother, you should show a little more respect", or something like that. I remember scoffing, and thinking that if their mother was so important, weren't the other mothers and fathers who died that day just as special. Why were they not on television, and why were the media not fawning over their extended families? It was disgraceful to me, that ordinary members of the public thought that they either knew Diana Spencer, or that they could somehow relate to her. The event was a non-event all in senses of the term. Simply put, two members of the jet set, one of them an heir to a department store fortune, the other a member of one of England's richest and most aristocratic families, and an ex member of the royal house, got into a car driven by a man who was over the limit and found to have been using prescription medication. Photographers on motorbikes followed them as they left the Paris Ritz hotel and the driver sped up, losing control of the vehicle as he entered the Pont de l'Alma tunnel. The resulting crash was enough to force the radiator of the Mercedes Benz the victims were travelling in, into the front seat, and unsurprisingly, three of the four passengers perished, them being Dodi Alfayed, Diana Spencer, and the driver Henri Paul. The bodyguard Trevor Rees-Jones was the only survivor. It was found by investigators that the responsibility of the crash lay with the driver and the driver alone, much to the consternation of the media, who sought blame where there was none. Now, you may wonder what this has to do with the monarchy, and my aversion to it, so please allow me to explain. The outpouring of grief and sentimentality of that week horrified me, and should have horrified you, not for the reasons normally given; that we had lost a great humanitarian, that she was young and beautiful, that she did so much for charity, etc, etc. What was chilling was the recruitment en masse of everyone into a single emotional mould, and is exactly the situation that we as a society do not want to find ourselves in. Whilst the accident was more or less meaningless, the aftermath was much more enlightening, and showed that it was possible for a single event to show the worst elements of society for everyone to see. For a good week or more after the death of Diana Spencer, the airwaves, television, and print were saturated with all sorts of nonsense, much of it extremely offensive to a great many people. The media, spearheaded by the BBC, decided that there was a national mood, and that everyone must share in this national mood. Other media outlets did not behave any better. The Daily Mail, that rag that a good many people read on a daily basis, still runs Diana Spencer stories, and was one of the worst newspapers for printing saccharine tales of how much the woman would be missed by everyone. It gleefully showed pictures of the mourning thousands, lining the streets and throwing tonnes (literally) of flowers into the path of the funeral procession and onto the roof of the hurst, yet, without irony, fourteen years later, the paper was openly mocking the North Korean people for weeping and howling in the streets when Kim Jong-Il died of a suspected heart attack, and even suggested that the public had been forced into displaying their grief. The hypocrisy that was shown by the media in the weeks leading up to the death and immediately after it was amazing to behold, and I don't think some of them ever got over it.

In another incredible display of hypocrisy, the public were heaping blame and ridicule on the paparazzi for being, as they saw it, involved in Diana's death, and then taking hundreds of thousands of pictures of the funeral procession and the mountains of flowers and bouquets on their cameras the next, seemingly not realising that they were engaging in the very activity which they had so lambasted only moments before.

Another troubling consequence of the paparazzi being blamed, perhaps not exclusively, for the death of Diana Spencer, is the willingness of the law to side again and again with the so called victims. This practice reared its ugly head recently when the now Duchess of Cambridge, Catherine

Middleton, sought and was given money for the fact that she was photographed by the media. She didn't want the attention it was said, and the photographers who had the audacity to photograph her, or at least the papers and magazines that they worked for, were forced to pay heavy fines. Now, you would have thought that an intelligent and switched on young woman, like Catherine Middleton evidently is, would have checked to see whether marrying into the royal family would have meant an increase in media attention before saying "I do", but this seems to have slipped her mind. Unless Catherine Middleton had been living under a rock for the previous twenty years, she would have known that marrying Prince William would result in massive interest from the media and the general population at large. I am immune to the celebrity culture, and find it both boring and tedious to have to hear about things that I care nothing about (which by the way, is the main reason that I do not watch television), but there are many people whose whole lives revolve around gossiping about the latest celebrity scandal. The royal family, and anyone marrying into it, should know this, and to plead otherwise is just foolishness on their part.

To conclude, the Diana episode is a lesson. It is a lesson that says that when people give up their critical thinking faculties, ordinary and not very special humans are elevated to a status far beyond they deserve. Diana could have been said to have done some work for charity, but there are many tens of thousands of people that do far more, and have been doing so for far longer than she ever did, who get no credit, and who toil in obscurity their entire lives. We can be sure of only one thing; those people who do carry out charity work, and who do not expect a camera to follow them around whilst they are doing it, cannot be said to be doing it for their own self promotion. I am afraid the same cannot be said for the woman in question here. Placing another human mammal on a pedestal that the rest of us supposedly cannot reach, is perhaps one of the most important factors that inhibits the move from a feudal system of government to a truly democratic republic, and the mindset that it produces is not good for the health of society. It is high time we started to judge peoples reputations by their actions, and not the other way around.

Part II

Arguments in favour

CHAPTER 9

Value for money

A price is something you get. A cost is something you lose.

- Lois McMaster Bujold

If I have failed to convince you, so far, that the monarchy is founded on immoral ideology, and that it is allied to religion and superstition, and that the hereditary principle is self evidently absurd, and that the origin of kingship is barbaric, and that the divine right to rule is fatuous, and that the powers they possess are too many, and that the effects on the intelligence and credulity of the public is harmful, and that there are a number of unworthy successors to the throne, then hopefully I can show how the most common arguments for keeping the monarchy are without merit.

The first argument that we will examine is that the royal family is good value for money. By value for money I mean that they cost little, and bring in more, either in terms of actual monetary value, or benefits in other means, like business, investment, etc. The actual cost of keeping the monarchy depends on who you ask, and which services are included, so it is actually quite difficult, perhaps impossible, to get a completely accurate sum. The official figure, £33.3 million pounds for the 2013/2014 fiscal year, used to be made up of many smaller amounts, but is now rolled into one single annual payment, known as the "sovereign support grant". However, this amount does not take into account many of the other costs associated with having a monarchy. The table shown next outlines the other undisclosed, estimated costs, and is taken from a report put together by Republic, a lobbying group in the United Kingdom that argues for the abolition of the monarchy.

Expenditure	Cost
Sovereign support grant	£33.3 million pounds
Annuity for Duke of Edinburgh	£0.4 million pounds
State buildings used by royal family	£30 million pounds
Duchy of Cornwall profits/gains - lost	£54.8 million pounds

Duchy of Lancaster profits/gains - lost	£35.5 million pounds
Royal Collection net surplus - lost	£9.8 million pounds
Cost of royal visits	£21.5 million pounds
Royal household pension scheme	£2.2 million pounds
Security	£102 million pounds
Costs met by government departments and the Crown Estate	£3.8 million pounds
Cost of Lord Lieutenants	£2.1 million pounds
Bona vacantia proceeds - Duchy of Cornwall	£0.3 million pounds
Bona vacantia proceeds - Duchy of Lancaster	£3.4 million pounds
Civil list pensions	£0.1 million pounds
Legal costs to maintain royal secrecy	£0.2 million pounds
	Total = £299.4 million pounds

So, as the table shows, with all of the additional costs added on, it brings the total to nearly ten times the official figure at £299.4 million pounds.

Republic has also compiled a list of the comparisons and equivalent cost of other areas of governmental spending, and found that the total cost of the monarchy is greater than or equal to the annual cost of:

14,000 newly qualified NHS nurses

13,000 police officers

Ministry of Defence spending on food (£195m)

Oxfordshire County Council's annual social care budget (£198m)

Department of Health spending on the Cancer Drugs Fund (£200m)

Central government support for medical research charities (£200m)

Furthermore, additional cuts and savings announced by the British Government as part of its deficit reduction plan include:

A reduction in Ministry of Justice budget (£210m)

A reduction in Sure Start funding (£200m)

Savings from changing the housing benefit system (£200m)

Savings from freeze in civil service recruitment (£190m)

As you can quite easily see, the yearly cost of running the monarchy is equivalent to many important ventures and social expenditures, and it surely becomes harder and harder to justify paying all that money for such a paltry return. Republic also looked at the cost of other monarchies in Europe, and again found that the amount that we pay is far higher than other people in other countries.

In addition to the money paid directly to the royal family via the Sovereign Support Grant, the royal house also has other ways of bringing in money. The two big sources are the Duchies of Lancaster and Cornwall. These are portfolios of land, property, and other assets, including farm land, historic buildings, land for development, and other ventures. It may surprise you to know, but the Duchies are not the personal property of the royal family. None of the monarchs are entitled to either the land or properties themselves or the revenue that is generated from it, but the money generated from these assets goes straight into the pockets of the Queen and of Prince Charles regardless. In the event that we were to transition to a republic, then the monies generated would go straight to the treasury to the benefit of all taxpayers.

In addition to the Duchies of Lancaster and Cornwall, there is another land and property portfolio known as the Crown Estate. The surplus revenue from this portfolio is managed on behalf of the Government, and is paid directly to the treasury every annum. It is said that the Queen surrenders this revenue to the country, helping in effect to subsidise the cost of the monarchy. However, the Crown Estate is not the personal property of the royal family and so this is patently false. The report from Republic explains how this situation came about:

> The source of the confusion comes from the fact that a small part of the existing Crown Estate portfolio was the property of the monarch before the end of the 18th century, when the king had responsibility for the expenses of civil government. But this changed once the state (the Crown) and the person of the monarch became separate during the reign of George III. Since then the Crown Estate has been the 'hereditary possessions of the Sovereign', not the personal possessions of the individual acting as Sovereign.

Because this arrangement has to be formally repeated at the outset of each reign, some monarchists assert that a new monarch could claim the revenue for themselves. In fact, this 'renewal' is a formality and was described in 1952 by Burke Trend, a senior Treasury official, as 'simply a historical relic from much earlier days'. If the monarchy were to disappear tomorrow, the Crown Estate would continue to do what it has always done for nearly one thousand years - provide income for the administration of this country.

It is an unfortunate fact that excuses are made and traditions are alluded to in favour of the monarchy by even those in the highest seats in government. Even if we cannot transition to a republic in the next few years or decades, it is clear that there needs to be some sort of financial reform, giving greater control of the royal house's finances to the government, to be in the better interests of the people. The following is a short list, taken from the report by Republic, of just some of the reforms that could potentially be made to the royal finances to make them more transparent, more fair, and bring greater accountability:

The government should set an annual fixed budget for the monarchy, to be managed by the government

Security costs to be made transparent and accountable

The costs of royal visits to be paid for out of the royal family's budget

All members of the royal family to follow the same tax laws as everyone else

The revenue from the Duchies of Lancaster and Cornwall to go to the Treasury

The monarchies finances to be examined by the National Audit Office as is the case with any other public organisation

The Crown Estate to be renamed the National Estate, and all revenues to go to the Treasury

After looking at all of the evidence concerning the cost and expenses of the royal family, you may have come to the conclusion that if the royal family paid their own way, or if they cost little to nothing in terms of the burden on the taxpayer, then my critique would fail. In this you would be wrong, as the main objections to there being a monarchy at all would still be valid, in that the hereditary principle is ridiculous, the powers they enjoy too many, and the undemocratic principles which reside behind all of their actions remain.

CHAPTER 10

Tradition, grandeur and charisma

Ritual will always mean throwing away something: destroying our corn or wine upon the altar of our gods.

- Gilbert K. Chesterton

One popular argument that is often employed in favour of keeping the royal house is that without them, who would provide the tradition, grandeur, and charisma that have become so integral to this country's identity? There is no doubt that watching trooping the colour, or seeing the guards standing tall in their reds, or the opening of parliament, is very impressive to some people, and brings a nostalgic tear to many an eye, but it is ridiculous in the extreme to think that this charade can and should go on forever. Is there any person alive that could say with a straight face that this type of behaviour will still be going on in another thousand years? Do you really believe, that after watching men and women set foot on the outer planets of our solar system, achieved with technology that will dwarf the kind that we have today, people will turn away from that awesome, majestic, mind expanding achievement, to look at a decaying relic from another time? Again, I leave the question open in your mind.

It is no secret that part of the draw of the United Kingdom for many tourists is the tradition and the history of our country, and I would be the first to admit that the monarchy has had a big hand in cultivating this view, regardless of if they have done this consciously or not. It is also true to say that many people around the world - North Americans for example - feel slightly empty when they think of their own history and traditions, mainly because it only goes back a few hundred years at the most, and that the traditions that they do have feel much less firmly rooted because of this fact. Our history is long enough for many of the traditions to be lost in a fog of uncertainty, which is why no doubt that the legends of King Arthur and Robin Hood sprung into being. By comparison, the entire history of the North American continent is well known and documented, and because of this, just seems to pop into existence a few hundred years ago. I would add, that just because we have a long and varied history, does not automatically mean that we should revere all of it, or that we should celebrate all of it. There are many instances in our own history that we would do better to learn from; the dark ages for example, or the crusades, or the burning of witches. Tradition is sometimes referenced as a get out of jail free card when it comes to practices that many people would find immoral today but for the fact that it is traditional. In moving to a republic, one of the great cultural endeavours will be working out which bits of our history and culture to keep and to continue, and which to throw out.

It is said that the monarchy provides something for the common man and woman to look up to, to revere, and to respect. To me, there is something very servile at the heart of this argument, as if we *need* someone to look up to, or as if our own lives are so worthless that we need to be occupied thinking about someone else's. This fanaticism reared its ugly head to a very large degree during the weddings of Charles and Diana, the death of Diana Spencer, and the recent marriage of Prince William and Kate Middleton. It is worth remembering that the cult of personality, and the cult of celebrity may not be as harmless as they first appear. We must also remember that the word "fan", is simply a shortened version of "fanatic". I have grown up admiring men and women who actually achieved things in their lives, and either improved the wellbeing of others around them, or expanded the outlook and knowledge of mankind. A moments thought here should conjure up images of Charles Darwin, Isaac Newton, Stephen Hawking, Richard Dawkins, Edwin Hubble, and Albert Einstein, and this is only to mention those that are involved in science and the understanding of the universe. It might be cheap to point out, but I have never read of any accomplishment by any royal family member that even comes close to discovering the expansion of the universe, or the laws of gravitational attraction.

The fact that many young people (and many adults as well come to think of it), do not know about the great discoveries that have been made by mankind is not the fault of the royal family by any means, and is, in my opinion at least, because of the gigantic flaw in our education system, that continually teaches not *how* to think, but *what* to think. The constant need by ministers, and by extension education chiefs, and by further extension parents, to make their children pass exams, has left us with young minds that do not know the difference between facts and theories, do not know how the scientific method came to be, and do not have even a basic grasp of many philosophical principles, which I would argue are essential for the formation of a critical and intelligent mind.

There are many people who maintain that without the monarchy we would lose a sense of identity, that without a monarch a politician would represent us overseas, and who would want that? I agree that some politicians are more than insufferable, and the idea of some of them representing us abroad I would find abhorrent, but at least they would be open to criticism from a foreign leader, and at least they would be on an equal footing with whomever they met with. This is simply not possible with the queen, as it does not matter who she meets, the person in question is expected to be deferent to her, not to speak before she does, and to keep their personal opinions private.

If the monarchy is said to give us a sense of identity, then surely this means that we must be able to identify with them, at least to some extent. But who can possibly identify with a person who is so absolutely singular? It is not even as though any normal member of the public has a chance of being in the monarchs position, and the queens day to day life is as different from the average persons as it is possible to imagine. This situation becomes even more untenable if we contrast it with the life of, say, a child living on the poverty line in a family relying on food banks for basic sustenance. Can anyone seriously argue that this child takes comfort from the fact that there is a monarchy, or that the monarch gives them a sense of identity?

As for the last point, which would be that the members of the royal family have charisma, I would argue that none of them have any of this, or at the very least, precious little of it. It is true that charisma can sometimes make us overlook certain moral shortcomings in people, but I would argue that this is not a desirable situation. This relates to the fact that, as I mention elsewhere, in our modern society the actions of many men and women in the pubic eye are judged by their reputations and not the other way about, and if this salient fact is ever going to change then we must not rely on charisma as the measure of human worth.

There is no doubt that humans have a tendency for ritual, but this is not necessarily something that should be encouraged or looked upon with fondness. Rituals and ritualistic behaviours come from the childhood of our species, when we were too ignorant of how the natural world actually worked, and would stupidly link multiple events that had nothing to do with each other, in order to either make them more understandable or to bring them under some sort of control, even if that control was illusory. Pomp and ceremony are just another relic of the past, which may have been useful once, but which now serve no purpose. Do not think that I am not respectful of tradition; it certainly has its place in less serious situations, and makes us feel more human and more connected to each other and the societies in which we dwell, but when it comes to the matter of human institutions that make decisions that affect us all, would it not make sense to strip out these antiquated ideas and start fresh, with nothing distracting the men and women whose job it is to try and figure out how to best run a successful society?

Tradition, grandeur and charisma are important for the cultural lifeblood of a country, in order to make us feel part of something bigger than ourselves, but in my opinion these things are not special enough to warrant the existence of the monarchy. Even if these three things could be said to be especially great as a direct result of there being a monarchy, this would still not come even close to rebutting the points I made in *Part I*, let alone being a positive reason for a monarchic system. In the event that we do transition to a republic, we will not lose something precious about ourselves that can never be replaced, but instead we will discover what is really important about our culture, and refine and hone it to an even greater degree. This process will not be painful, but rather enjoyable, as without the constant blare and din of royalist horn blowing and drumbeating we will rediscover english language and literature, we will again appreciate and admire the great scientific minds that we are lucky enough to call our countrymen, and we can look forward to other earth shattering achievements by future generations, without the interruption of royal weddings, jubilees, and other tawdry, unimportant events.

CHAPTER 11

Charity

Charity is injurious unless it helps the recipient to
become independent of it.
                                    - John D. Rockefeller

The third most popular argument for the
continuation of the royal family is that of charity,
and the fact that they do so much for various causes
both in this country and abroad. This is a valid
point and deserves analysis.

With regards to the rise of charity work
being carried out by the monarchy, it is thought to
have started with the first recorded patronage of
George II's involvement with the Society of
Antiquaries, an institution that concerned itself with
architectural and art history, conservation and
heraldry. This no doubt was seen by many at the
time as a noble thing to do, but these are kings and
queens we are talking about here. Are they serious
when they suggest that the first area of concern

when it was thought that the monarch should lend his name and support to an organisation was that of the fate of buildings, paintings, and other relics? Even with my limited intellect I can think of many causes that would have been much more worthy of charity.

At the heart of all of the monarchy's charitable work is a very real demon that must be met head on. I am talking about the hypocritical nature by which on the one hand the royals exist to a large degree by the generosity of the taxpayer, which must mean that they do not have to work for a living like the majority of the rest of the population, and the applauding of the people for their ability to perform charitable work. As an example of this, Prince William's professed concern for the homelessness situation in the capital and other areas of the country would perhaps be a little easier to take seriously if we did not hear that the home that him and his wife will occupy, an apartment in Kensington Palace, will need at least £4 million pounds worth of work to make into a habitable state.

It has been noted that the charities that the various members of the royal family get involved with are normally ones in which they have an interest, again proving that the human characteristic of bias is very real, even in people who are supposed to have none and be above politics. It must also be noted that every celebrity of any worth has a signature charity, or at least one that they do a lot of work with. Now, it is impossible to say whether every single one of those people really care for the objects of their charity, or if they are simply doing it because it is good for public relations and the improvement of their image. My bet is that there are a huge number that do it for the benefit of their careers and also a large number that do it for the betterment of mankind. The end result could be said to be the same however, in that even the most self-centred and egotistical person who actually does charity work is helping others, even if it is for the wrong reasons. If a film star pays for some school to be built in some backwater part of Africa, and only does it for the advancement of their career and some publicity, at the end of it all the school has still been built. I have not got a problem with this, as long as the person in question is honest about their reasons for doing so. It is my opinion that the hypocrisy is much worse than the lie in the first instance. The average person on the street may well do things for charity, but they have to do this in their spare time, or give up a proportion of their money they have earned directly to the cause they care about. Who is to say that given unlimited resources and time, and not having to work for a living, many of these selfless people would not devote their lives to helping others? The answer is that there is no quantitative way to know this. There are in fact many people around the world that work tirelessly for the downtrodden and those more unfortunate than themselves, and I have every trust that this would continue no matter what happened to us as a species.

A very common problem, as I have mentioned already, is that far too often peoples actions are judged by their reputations, and not the other way around. Many people in the public eye are simply well known for being well known, which, I submit, is not a state of affairs we should be pleased about being in. As it turns out, there is a member of the royal family who does do huge amounts for charity, and apparently does so with the intention of making the peoples lives she touches better. I am not talking about the deceased disco princess, but Princess Anne. Here is a woman who has been the patron of the save the children foundation for over twenty five years, but is never in the news, is rarely in the media, and is never featured in photo opportunities. The reason is probably quite simple, in that she is not photogenic, compared to Diana Spencer, who it has to be said, was a very attractive young woman. This either shows that the public does not really care about the real charity work that goes on, which could well be true, or that it only matters that charity work is done by attractive people who look like they actually care about it, even if in private they do not. This is not a problem that is caused by the royal family, but rather of the media and the population as a whole. If the media did not take these types of pictures, and if the public did not want them, then that would be the end of it. You must realise that I am not disputing the work done by the royal family for charity for a single instance; any amount of research will show that they do many things and support many good causes both here and in other countries around the world, but it surely must matter whether or not they want to do these things or whether they have to do them.

Another question is this; what exactly would the royal family do if it were not for charity work? We know that some of the royals serve in the armed forces, which is admirable, but which still raises some questions of promotion, heredity, and other problems, but this is a small percentage of the total royal house. I think the answer is that as the role of the monarch has changed, and they have had their powers stripped a little, they have been blessed, or cursed, depending on your view, with more and more free time, in which something for them to do had to be found. The whole reason that the aims and actions of the monarchy have changed over the years is because the zeitgeist has changed too much for them to be able to remain the same. As I have said elsewhere, the job of the monarch in the early days of our society was not to perform charity work; it was *Defender of the Faith*, and it was to resolve disputes, order and fight in wars, and to act where only his or or her power was believed to be adequate for the task at hand. Now that the powers, even though still numerous and far reaching, have been culled a little, this job description has had to change out of necessity.

To close this chapter, I put forward a challenge: if the royal house are genuinely, passionately interested in charity, then the members of that family should all abdicate, sell off any possessions that they have inherited or have been given by the state, and redirect the monies generated to the charities of their, perhaps I should say our, choice. In addition, the revenues from the Duchies of Lancaster and Cornwall should go towards helping the poor and disadvantaged of this country, and the money saved from having a royal family, which is approximately £300 million pounds per year, should go someway to providing a very high standard of education for the children of this country indefinitely. This way, even I could come close to considering forgiving the monarchy for imposing themselves on our culture and society for so long, they could bow out with dignity, and be remembered for something very much different than they currently are.

CHAPTER 12

Tourism

Worth seeing? Yes; but not worth going to see.
- Samuel Johnson

One of the more unimaginative arguments for keeping the monarchy is that the institution brings in lots of money from tourism. Now you have to admit, going from being put in power by the creator of the universe to simply being good for tourism seems to be quite a drop in standards, and indeed it is. I could if I wanted to, and I am tempted, to leave it right there, already just having shown the absolute absurdity of the tourism argument, but as I am aiming for a thorough critique, this means that we should look at all of the issues, no matter how meaningless we might believe them to be. Let's ignore the fact that the original mandate for one person or family ruling over the rest of us was divine in nature, as I have already exhaustively debunked in an earlier chapter, and concentrate on exactly how much money interest in the royal family generates. VisitBritain have estimated that the royals are responsible for bringing in around £500 million pounds every year as a direct result of tourism. Their argument was that many of the attractions in the UK are connected to the royal family in some way, therefore if there was not a monarchy in place then this figure of £500 million would fall. Now, I agree with most people, in saying that half a billion pounds is a substantial sum of money, however, in 2012 the total revenue generated from all tourism was estimated to be £134 billion, taken from a report by Tourism Alliance, an organisation that represents a huge number of tourist agencies. If the £500 million supposedly brought into the country by monarchy related tourism is to be taken at face value, then it only represents around 0.37% of the total revenue brought into the country as a result of tourism. By the way that the royalists go on, you would have thought that the figure would be much, much higher, and remember, this is only if we take the £500 million estimated by VisitBritain as factually verifiable. The likelihood is that the £500 million figure put forward is not accurate, resulting in an even lower overall percentage of revenue from royal tourists.

In order to get an idea of what tourists actually visit these islands for, it is worth looking at a partial list from The Association of Leading Visitor Attractions, whose organisation puts together a list every year of the biggest draws for tourists. The table that follows shows the top 20 tourist attractions in the UK for 2013, including total visits, whether the attraction is free of charge or carries a cost, and whether the number of visitors has increased or decreased as compared with the year before.

Rank	Site	Total visits	Free/ Charge	% +/-
1	British Museum	6,701,036	F/C	20
2	National Gallery	6,031,574	F/C	14
3	Natural History Museum	5,356,884	F/C	6.7
4	Tate Modern	4,884,939	F/C	-8
5	Science Museum	3,316,000	F/C	10.9
6	V&A	3,290,500	F/C	1.8
7	Tower of London	2,984,698	C	18.4

8	Somerset House Trust	2,398,066	F/C	N/C
9	St Paul's Cathedral	2,138,130	F/C	19
10	Westminster Abbey	2,020,637	F/C	13.8
11	National Portrait Gallery	2,014,636	F/C	-4
12	Old Royal Naval College Greenwich	1,803,477	F	1
13	National Museum of Scotland	1,768,090	F/C	-7
14	British Library	1,475,382	F/C	4.3
15	National Maritime Museum	1,437,725	F/C	27
16	Edinburgh Castle	1,420,027	F/C	15
17	Chester Zoo	1,409,249	F/C	0
18	Tate Britain	1,378,272	F/C	-10

19	Royal Botanic Gardens Kew	1,324,499	C	29.4
20	ZSL London Zoo	1,294,483	C	26.4

As you can quite easily see from this table, none of the top 20 tourist attractions have much to do with the royal family, let alone being one of their official residences. In fact, at the time of writing, Windsor Castle would come in at number 24 on the list above, with official visitors numbers in the 900,000's. If the line that the royals are important for tourism is to be accepted without question, then it is surprising that many of the people who supposedly come here precisely because of the monarchy, are simply visiting other sites that have little or nothing to do with the institution itself.

Another fallacy is committed when it is assumed that the people that visit the tourist attractions associated with the monarchy would not do so if there were no monarchy. A single moments thought cuts through this premise. If we take Buckingham Palace as an example, large swathes of it are completely off limits to members of the public and tourists, and are never opened for viewing, and tours do not run all of the time. Surely more money would be generated if the entire building was opened up, and a museum was created out of the remnants of the dynasty. It is known that Buckingham Palace is only open for 8 weeks of the year, and manages to attract visitor numbers in the 400,000's. Is it too much to imagine that if opened all year round the attraction would not generate much more revenue than it currently does? It is also commonly thought, or at least guessed, that most of the royal tourists come to get a glimpse of their favourite royal. In reality this is a near impossibility, unless there is an official event going on at the time, or their visit happens to coincide with a state event such as a jubilee, marriage, birth, or death.

We must also remember that tourists do not get to see any of the royals when they visit these attractions, much less interact with them. So, in effect, they are visiting for the history, the architecture, and to learn something of the place. Buildings like Buckingham Palace and Windsor Castle would undoubtedly become more popular if they were open longer hours and visitors had access to many parts of the buildings that were previously denied to them. This is exactly what has happened in the case of the Louvre in Paris, where the art and other attractions bring in many millions of people per year and generate far more money for the surrounding economy than Buckingham Palace could ever hope for.

The question that needs answering is the following: do tourists come to this country and visit the royal residences in the hope of getting a glimpse, even a slight one, of one of the members of the royal family? Or are they simply here to get photographs of the buildings, the monuments, and the historic sights that are aligned to the monarchy? It would be easy to answer this question, if we do a small thought experiment. If, as I maintain is true, that tourists rarely, if ever, get to see any member of the royal family, then what would be different if the royal family did have to pack its bags and go? Would the said tourists now stop visiting and taking pictures of Buckingham Palace, Kensington Palace, and the Tower of London? Contrary to what the royalists say, tourism numbers and the money brought into the country would probably increase in the event that our country became a republic, because the sites that are normally closed and off limits to the public would instead be open all year round with no restriction on areas that could be visited, photographed, or experienced.

To summarise, even though we have examined the claim that the royal family are responsible for attracting huge numbers of tourists to this country and have found it to be vacuous, and have declared that the tourists do not have any real chance of seeing the royals themselves, and in reality come for the history of our country and the incredible architecture, and that opening the monuments and palaces fully and all year round would generate many times more revenue than they currently do, it would not matter even if we did *not* come to these conclusions. If it could be conclusively proven that the monarchy were responsible for bringing hundreds of millions of pounds into the country as a direct result of tourism, and that this was then put forward as a good enough reason for keeping them, then the royalists are in effect saying that our democratic rights are for sale. I have been brought up to believe that principles matter, and for me those principles include the right to elect those within whom I put my trust to run the country. At this moment in time, in this country at least, I cannot do this. I have no say in who the next monarch will be, and no say whether there is a monarchy or not, save for writing this pamphlet and keeping the argument alive, and for me it is not worth giving that up for a few hundred million pounds. Other people in this country may have their price, but I do not.

CHAPTER 13

Other arguments

"A dying monarchy is always one that has too much power, not too little; a dying religion always interferes more than it ought, not less."
- G. K. Chesterton

To finish our look at the most common arguments that are professed by royalists, we now turn and examine some of the less common but still valid objections to moving to a republican government.

One objection to getting rid of the monarchy is that it would be replaced by a presidential system, which will be even more unbearable than having a monarchy. These critics seem not to realise that if we do replace the royal house with a republic we are free to choose exactly how the system works. If you do not want to see a presidential system that is similar to the United States then there is nothing that says we have to. If you do not want the system to become too ritualistic, as it could be argued that the U.S. system is becoming or has become, then that is fine, as it is well within our powers to set up a system of government that does not do this and does not make the mistakes that others have done.

There is no doubt that it is part of the human condition to make things unnecessarily ritualistic, perhaps because, as many anthropologists have discovered, important moments in ones life often mean more, or are more memorable, if there is some modicum of ritual associated with it. I think that it is in our best interests, if and when we do move to a republican system, to remove all forms of ritual, pomp, and ceremony from the political system, no matter how much we might like to keep them there for our own gratification. I am not saying that life should be a miserable shuffle from the womb to the grave, but that the means of governing the lives of all of us should be as transparent and unemotional as possible, for the sake of all of our interests. It is also my opinion that by allowing ritualistic behaviours into the governmental system that those directly involved in it become slightly more credulous. Not by much perhaps, but it must still have an effect, and as the best way to derive policy is by examining and then acting upon evidence, any behaviours that reinforce faith and belief without evidence must be limited.

The critics of the presidential system, or those that think that we will be left with a President Blair, seem to think that if we move to a republic that the people will not have a choice in the matter. Many people lament the fact that George Bush got into power, but the fact remains that the people of the United States voted for him, and they voted for every other person that has become Commander in Chief. They are also free, and have exercised the power, to remove certain presidents by impeachment. I would agree that the calibre of presidential candidates has dropped in recent years, and that the campaign finance system across the atlantic is completely corrupt and in need of a thorough redesign, but we have the chance to correct all of these things before they even become an issue. In short, the solution would be to take all of the best characteristics from other states and governments and combine them into one that is uniquely our own. I do not think that this situation is entirely outside the scope of our abilities, but the only way to find out if it is, is by actually trying it.

An objection that is not very common but is put forward nonetheless, is that the countries that do not have a monarchy are sometimes much worse off for not having one. There are numerous examples that are normally cited, but the problem is that the initial premise is mistaken. Yes, of course, societies like Somalia and Afghanistan are failed, and have been failing for a very long time, but it is not because they do not have monarchies that they are struggling to thrive. In the case of Afghanistan they did actually have a monarchy, and many people in that country yearn for the days when they did have someone who was in ultimate power. But theocracy, as Afghanistan descended into, is not the only alternative to monarchy, and it is simply untrue to say that we would be worse off if we did transition to a republic. We must remember that the monarchy is not what defines this country, even if many people around the world think this to be the case.

The last argument that we will examine, and one that I actually think is the hardest to address, at least in my mind, is the fact that many people are simply not that interested in politics, or how their country is run, until it starts to affect them personally or financially. Many people that I have spoken to feel that the royal family and their goings on have so little impact on their lives that it is pointless worrying about them. I am inclined to agree, even though I do not like to admit it. Why would the average working man or woman, perhaps struggling to put food on the table and to keep their head above the poverty line, care enough to read a pamphlet like the one you are reading now? If they do not feel that the existence of the royal family has any bearing on their day to day lives, then why on earth would they interest themselves in the argument to either abolish or keep the monarchy?

In addition, many people simply do not think about it enough. They are not curious about any of the topics that I have raised so far, and I have a feeling that nothing that I say or do will have an effect on this either. It is not an exaggeration to say that a large proportion of the population would have a monarchy, even if it inconvenienced them, just as long as there was a jubilee to celebrate, or a royal wedding to obsess over every few years. As I have already said, this attitude is not a dangerous one in and of itself, and is not a threat to civilisation at this very moment in time, but who is to say that there will not be someone who comes along in a few years or decades that is not so innocent, and seeks to impose their views on the populace at large via the secrecy that the monarchic system currently affords. In that case, it will be too late to object, as it always is when tyrannies are finally revealed for their true nature. These things do not happen overnight, and are instead inculcated by slow, meandering methods, until such time as when the switch is finally thrown, the illumination that results is all the more horrifying.

To summarise, there are many arguments for keeping a monarchy that do not come close to reaching the level of importance that the earlier arguments I have covered attain, but this does not necessarily mean that they are without merit. If the people do not care enough to fight against the very thing that is the source of the injustice, then realistically there is little that can be done until the mindset of the people is changed. This will not be a quick process, but rather will rely on a slow, steady dissemination of information, prose, and polemic, that will, over time, move the zeitgeist to a position that is more favourable to the republican cause.

Part III

Building a Republic

CHAPTER 14

A better tradition

Name a society that based its precepts on the ideas of Newton, Darwin, Lucretius, Democritus, Plato, Socrates, Spinoza, Einstein, Thomas Jefferson, and Thomas Paine, and then turned to beggary, bankruptcy, and ruin.

- Christopher Hitchens

As we now have examined in detail the specific problems with the monarchic system, and the ways in which the most common arguments for the institution are fatuous, the next stage of our critique is to answer those who would question how we would proceed. How would we build the republic that I am so ardently calling for? How would we make the transition? And would our society, after all of the pain and strife that it may experience in getting there, be better off in the end?

Perhaps the most worrying aspect of moving from a monarchy to a democratic republic, at least for those who are firmly in the royalist camp, is what will happen to the sense of tradition, grandeur, and history that is so often put forward as an argument for keeping the institution in the first place. The royalists I have spoken to genuinely believe that without the figurehead of the monarch we will be cast off and left adrift, and simply bounce from one vacuous president to the next, losing our sense of national pride and identity, and all the while looking back to a time when there was something to look up to, or someone up to which to look. There is also the belief, that in my mind is more widespread than first appearances may let on, that the culture of english language and literature, science and reason, and the enlightened individuals that we have produced, is somehow too elitist for the ordinary man or woman to get emotional about or attached to in any meaningful way. In this respect I could not disagree more, as many of the most brilliant minds came from humble and modest backgrounds, were not educated traditionally or at a high level, and made the best of their situation and succeeded regardless of their upbringing. This is in stark contrast to the extremely privileged upbringing that even run of the mill members of the royal family enjoy, and I repeat, not a single one of them has ever done anything that remotely justifies the deference paid to them.

Just take a minute to think of the contribution that the men and women of this country have made to not just our society and culture, but to that of many societies and cultures around the world. We have english language and literature, and the contributions from science and technology. This is the country that gave the world Isaac Newton, Charles Darwin, and Stephen Hawking, and the mind expanding and earth shattering discoveries that they made. Are you seriously suggesting that these great men are lesser than a group of people that have never done anything remarkable, in the hundreds of years that they have been in power?

Although the United States seems to have slipped a little in intellectual standards, especially in the last few years, it nevertheless remains a place of great learning, and in my opinion we should all learn a lesson from the specific way in which the United States was founded. There is no doubt that the United States was lucky when she received Thomas Paine, Joseph Priestley, and many other minds of the enlightenment, after they were driven out by either the idea of the monarchy, or simply sought a new and prosperous place to keep expanding their minds and make a difference to the world, and it is no accident that both of those men ended up in Philadelphia, which was a serious centre for learning. The fact that these men were able to write and speak as they did, and bring about the most successful revolution in history, and one that still endures to this day, is testament to the brilliance of their minds and their intellect. Yet for many North Americans, to know of Thomas Jefferson, Benjamin Franklin, Thomas Paine, and others, is not as common as it should be. The lack of respect or ignorance, at least on a much larger societal scale, for the figures that I have mentioned already, is one of many things about our society and others around the world that is in need of change. I am not saying that all school children need to be inculcated with the names of great scientists and philosophers, but it would not be a poorer society if we educated young minds in the importance and beauties of science, the arts, literature, and a love of learning and knowledge, rather than the rote recitation of facts and figures such as they are exposed to today. Obviously this would require a lot of work, and changing the education system from the inside out would require more than a short chapter in a book of this kind, but nevertheless it is something that will have to be carried out at some point if we are to build a society of any merit.

So, how would we transition from a constitutional monarchy to a purely democratic republic? I am not a political science graduate, and in my opinion there is no need to be one to comment on these things, but surely it cannot be too difficult to move from what we have now to something that would be better for all of us. As for the actual action of the abolishment of the monarchy there are a number of different views here. Thomas Paine tried in vain to persuade the French not to execute their king, if only because he thought that starting a revolution with an act of capital punishment would send the wrong message, and only ensures that an original sin is committed that is then extremely hard to absolve. In one way it would be satisfying to simply force the monarchs to pack their bags and to just let them get on with their own lives, just as the rest of us must do, but this would only be rewarding in the short term, and would not achieve any real benefit. It would be better if, when the time comes for them to fold their tents and go, that they volunteer to do so, and leave with dignity. I certainly would not think less of them if the royal family did do this, and in fact my level of respect for them would immediately jump up a few notches. They are lucky enough to be in the position to be able to enact some serious change, not just monetarily but also socially as well. Imagine if, when the current queen dies, that it is announced by the extended royal family that the time of their dynasty is over, and they are going to devote the rest of their lives to the causes that they already engage in, without relying on the taxpayer to foot the bill, and without all of the pomp and ceremony that come with being part of the royal family.

To summarise, we do not have to despair at which route our society will take if and when we do transition to a republican system of government. We have greater minds, we have greater tenacity, and we have greater resolve than many other nations put together, and have come through some of the most difficult experiences with our integrity intact. We have the words and writings of some of the greatest minds that have ever lived to look back upon, and there is no reason to think that Britain's future will not be just as bright. The abolishment of the monarchy is a necessary precursor to ensuring that this future happens.

CHAPTER 15

A Declaration

> Many a revolution started with the actions of a few.
> Only fifty six men signed the Declaration of
> Independence. A few hanging together can lead a
> nation to change.
>
> - Wynton Marsalis

It is not hyperbole to say that humans have been on this planet long enough to know exactly what constitutes a successful society and what doesn't. It is no surprise to any morally serious human being that the Taliban are not successful in their attempts to create and run a pluralistic society. We can examine their efforts and find the ways in which they govern and the methods by which they impose laws to be an anathema to human wellbeing. Too often, in this country at least, many people are quick to dismiss the alternative society that we could build if we were to transition to a republic. Images of simpering and smug politicians are usually conjured up, with the optional "President

Blair", or "President Thatcher" remark. It does not have to be this way, as we will have the right to vote for whomever we like when and if we did ever move to a more democratic system. The most obvious example to point to would be the United States of America. The United States has a large number of social problems, as does any country, but is there really a more plural and more inclusive place on earth? Can you name me any society that has a bigger range of ethnic groups, ideological viewpoints, and the greatest range of freedom, both in terms of speech and of the press? I certainly cannot.

It may seem like the United States is a very religious and intolerant place, but this is an image that is more stereotypical than anything else. Yes, the majority of North Americans are religious, and more specifically various denominations of Christian, but on paper the United States is a purely secular country. The constitution is godless, and even though it was written by deists and theists, they knew that the only way to stop persecution of any religious group by another was to have a secular constitution, and even now, this is still the only method of government that can possibly claim to be able to do this, all others being unable to by definition.

The Declaration of Independence, part of which I show next, was drawn up by some of the greatest minds of its day, and is a landmark document for many reasons. It lays out, concisely and devastatingly, the case against the King of England, George III, for why the United States should be independent, and is not surprisingly considered one of the most important pieces of writing ever produced. I have left out the introduction and the preamble, but have reproduced the objections in full, for the usefulness of our critique, and to show, once again, that even though our current monarch may not abuse the powers that she has been invested with (that we know of), the system itself will always allow the potential for abuses to occur.

> The history of the present King of Great Britain is a history of repeated injuries and usurpations, all having in direct object the establishment of an absolute Tyranny over these States. To prove this, let Facts be submitted to a candid world.
>
> He has refused his Assent to Laws, the most wholesome and necessary for the public good.
>
> He has forbidden his Governors to pass Laws of immediate and pressing importance, unless suspended in their operation till his Assent should be obtained; and when so suspended, he has utterly neglected to attend to them.

He has refused to pass other Laws for the accommodation of large districts of people, unless those people would relinquish the right of Representation in the Legislature, a right inestimable to them and formidable to tyrants only.

He has called together legislative bodies at places unusual, uncomfortable, and distant from the depository of their public Records, for the sole purpose of fatiguing them into compliance with his measures.

He has dissolved Representative Houses repeatedly, for opposing with manly firmness his invasions on the rights of the people.

He has refused for a long time, after such dissolutions, to cause others to be elected; whereby the Legislative powers, incapable of Annihilation, have returned to the People at large for their exercise; the State remaining in the mean time exposed to all the dangers of invasion from without, and convulsions within.

He has endeavoured to prevent the population of these States; for that purpose obstructing the Laws for Naturalisation of Foreigners; refusing to pass others to encourage their migrations hither, and raising the conditions of new Appropriations of Lands.

He has obstructed the Administration of Justice, by refusing his Assent to Laws for establishing Judiciary powers.

He has made Judges dependent on his Will alone, for the tenure of their offices, and the amount and payment of their salaries.

He has erected a multitude of New Offices, and sent hither swarms of Officers to harass our people, and eat out their substance.

He has kept among us, in times of peace, Standing Armies without the Consent of our legislatures.

He has affected to render the Military independent of and superior to the Civil power.

He has combined with others to subject us to a jurisdiction foreign to our constitution, and unacknowledged by our laws; giving his Assent to their Acts of pretended Legislation:

For Quartering large bodies of armed troops among us:

For protecting them, by a mock Trial, from punishment for any Murders which they should commit on the Inhabitants of these States:

For cutting off our Trade with all parts of the world:

For imposing Taxes on us without our Consent:

For depriving us in many cases, of the benefits of Trial by Jury:

For transporting us beyond Seas to be tried for pretended offences

For abolishing the free System of English Laws in a neighbouring Province, establishing therein an Arbitrary government, and enlarging its Boundaries so as to render it at once an example and fit instrument for introducing the same absolute rule into these Colonies:

For taking away our Charters, abolishing our most valuable Laws, and altering fundamentally the Forms of our Governments:

For suspending our own Legislatures, and declaring themselves invested with power to legislate for us in all cases whatsoever.

He has abdicated Government here, by declaring us out of his Protection and waging War against us.

He has plundered our seas, ravaged our Coasts, burnt our towns, and destroyed the lives of our people.

He is at this time transporting large Armies of foreign Mercenaries to complete the works of death, desolation and tyranny, already begun with circumstances of Cruelty & perfidy scarcely paralleled in the most barbarous ages, and totally unworthy of the Head of a civilised nation.

He has constrained our fellow Citizens taken Captive on the high Seas to bear Arms against their Country, to become the executioners of their friends and Brethren, or to fall themselves by their Hands.

He has excited domestic insurrections amongst us, and has endeavoured to bring on the inhabitants of our frontiers, the merciless Indian Savages, whose known rule of warfare, is an undistinguished destruction of all ages, sexes and conditions.

In every stage of these Oppressions We have Petitioned for Redress in the most humble terms:

Our repeated Petitions have been answered only by repeated injury. A Prince whose character is thus marked by every act which may define a Tyrant, is unfit to be the ruler of a free people. Nor have We been wanting in attentions to our British brethren. We have warned them from time to time of attempts by their legislature to extend an unwarrantable jurisdiction over us. We have reminded them of the circumstances of our emigration and settlement here. We have appealed to their native justice and magnanimity, and we have conjured them by the ties of our common kindred to disavow these usurpations, which, would inevitably interrupt our connections and correspondence. They too have been deaf to the voice of justice and of consanguinity. We must, therefore, acquiesce in the necessity, which denounces our Separation, and hold them, as we hold the rest of mankind, Enemies in War, in Peace Friends.

I think you will agree that the indictment was scathing in both its language and content, and in my opinion the founding fathers had no other choice but to announce independence. The document clearly makes it possible for a number of things to happen, the main one being that once the tyranny and oppression of the crown had been revealed and described, that it left open the possibility to examine what was wrong with the monarchical system, and replace it with something infinitely more just and plural. It is my intention to attempt the same thing here, in listing the misdeeds and infringements on our freedoms and liberty that the monarchic system and the hereditary principle have placed upon us, and to draw from that a similar document aimed at releasing us from the chains that they bind us with. It is important that this document not be aimed at an individual, as the Declaration of Independence was at King George III, but rather at the principles behind the royal institution itself. It is only by doing this that the document will be forever relevant, and will ensure that it does not simply apply to a specific time and place. What follows is the Declaration of the Republic of England.

Declaration of the Republic of England

It has become the purpose of the people of England, and those in affected member states around the world, to renounce the monarchic system and the hereditary principle, and to announce the reasons for doing so.

We hold the following truths to be self-evident, that all humans are born equal, that they are endowed by virtue of their existence with certain unalienable rights, that among these are life, liberty, and the pursuit of happiness.

To ensure the promulgation and continuation of these rights, the governments of mankind must derive their powers from the consent of the governed. When the long train of abuses, mental, physical, societal, cultural, logical, and reasonable, are realised, it is the right and duty of the people to throw off such rule, and to put in place new safeguards to protect themselves and their government.

The history of the current monarchic system is a history of repeated injuries and usurpations, and must be repudiated for the following reasons:

It rewards blood instead of merit, placing heredity before ability

It makes prisoners of the monarchs and serfs of the people

It insists on a divine right to rule without any evidence of the divine

It puts faith above reason, and is an antidote to evidence based policy

It gives powers not enjoyed by elected representatives to individuals put in power by heredity

It fosters ignorance, deference, credulity, and serfdom amongst the people

It ensures unworthy characters are placed in the highest positions of power

We will not be quiet on this fact. Reason itself rebels against faith, logic itself discredits heredity, intelligence upsets ignorance, pride abolishes serfdom, self worth negates deference, and enlightenment values trump all others.

We, therefore, the people of England and the commonwealth states, appealing to none other than our own reason, solemnly publish and declare, that we, as a people, are absolved from all allegiance and deference to the crown, and that all political connection between them and the government of the people be dissolved, and that as a government of the people, have the power to levy war, announce peace, contract alliances, establish commerce, and do all other acts and things that a peoples government has the right to do.

It is only after a document of this kind has been accepted and promulgated that we can start to build a society that is truly successful. Like the American example though, the journey would only start there. We are fortunate, in that many of our institutions and systems of government would stay much as they are, minus the interference from the crown in matters that do not concern them. It would be naive to think that we could progress without any changes however, and perhaps the most important next step would be to outline what a Bill of Rights should include, which I will endeavour to do in the next chapter.

To conclude, the need for a document that states plainly why we should move from a constitutional monarchy to a republic is obvious. It states the peoples intent, that the monarchy is not a system of government that can possibly have the best interests of the people at heart, and the reason for why the monarchic system cannot coexist with a modern democratic society.

CHAPTER 16

A Bill of Rights

A Bill of Rights is what the people are entitled to against every government, and what no just government should refuse, or rest on inference.
- Thomas Jefferson

Once a declaration has been made of the intent of the people to abstain from the practice of deference to either a single person who can be called the monarch, or the extended family of the said monarch, the next stage would be to outline a set of rights that enshrine in it many of the principles and freedoms that we should enjoy. It is often said that in the United Kingdom we have a certain number of unwritten rights, which simply means that instead of a single document detailing exactly what our rights are, they are contained within many different documents from many different periods in history. Even if we do not manage to rid ourselves of the monarchy, it is long overdue that we have a single document that lays out our rights, that would detail the responsibilities that we would have to one another, and that society would have to the individual. Obviously this is no place to start putting together a legal document, and even if I were adequately educated and qualified to do so, legalese is hardly interesting, and besides, the main points I wish to raise in this penultimate chapter are to do with the reasons why we need a bill of rights, and not specifically the rights themselves, except for specific examples.

To begin our examination of this subject, and to draw some vital inspiration, it is worth looking at some examples of bills of rights and other thinking on the subject. The first document that we are going to examine is the first ten amendments to the United States Constitution, that at the time were not, but later became, the Bill of Rights as they are known today. Again, as I did with the Declaration of Independence, I will reproduce here the entire list of ten amendments, so that we can get a clear idea of exactly what we are dealing with.

First Amendment - Congress shall make no law respecting an establishment of religion, or prohibiting the free exercise thereof; or abridging the freedom of speech, or of the press; or the right of the people peaceably to assemble, and to petition the Government for a redress of grievances.

Second Amendment - A well regulated Militia, being necessary to the security of a free State, the right of the people to keep and bear Arms, shall not be infringed.

Third Amendment - No Soldier shall, in time of peace be quartered in any house, without the consent of the Owner, nor in time of war, but in a manner to be prescribed by law.

Fourth Amendment - The right of the people to be secure in their persons, houses, papers, and effects, against unreasonable searches and seizures, shall not be violated, and no Warrants shall issue, but upon probable cause, supported by Oath or affirmation, and particularly describing the place to be searched, and the persons or things to be seized.

Fifth Amendment - No person shall be held to answer for a capital, or otherwise infamous crime, unless on a presentment or indictment of a Grand Jury, except in cases arising in the land or naval forces, or in the Militia, when in actual service in time of War or public danger; nor shall any person be subject for the same offence to be twice put in jeopardy of life or limb; nor shall be compelled in any criminal case to be a witness against himself, nor be deprived of life, liberty, or property, without due process of law; nor shall private property be taken for public use, without just compensation.

Sixth Amendment - In all criminal prosecutions, the accused shall enjoy the right to a speedy and public trial, by an impartial jury of the State and district wherein the crime shall have been committed, which district shall have been previously ascertained by law, and to be informed of the nature and cause of the accusation; to be confronted with the witnesses against him; to have compulsory process for obtaining witnesses in his favour, and to have the Assistance of Counsel for his defence.

Seventh Amendment - In suits at common law, where the value in controversy shall exceed twenty dollars, the right of trial by jury shall be preserved, and no fact tried by a jury, shall be otherwise re-examined in any court of the United States, than according to the rules of the common law.

Eighth Amendment - Excessive bail shall not be required, nor excessive fines imposed, nor cruel and unusual punishments inflicted.

Ninth Amendment - The enumeration in the Constitution, of certain rights, shall not be construed to deny or disparage others retained by the people.

Tenth Amendment - The powers not delegated to the United States by the Constitution, nor prohibited by it to the States, are reserved to the States respectively, or to the people.

As the ten amendments are not exceedingly long it is possible to break their core meaning down into a few lines, and that is what I will do next.

The first amendment simply ensures the freedom of speech of any citizen, the freedom of the press, the right to assemble, and also the freedom to worship or not.

The second amendment describes the right of the citizen to bear arms, which can be understood in the time and place of the revolution, but which is still valid today.

The third amendment guards against the forced quartering of troops, and came about as the result of the British forcing the colonists to house and feed British troops.

The fourth amendment protects the citizen against unreasonable searches and seizures.

The fifth amendment simply guarantees a trial by jury, guards against double jeopardy, and also self-incrimination.

The sixth amendment guarantees the rights of the accused, including a speedy and public trial, the right to be informed of the charges made against him, the right to call witnesses in his defence, and the right to have an attorney.

The seventh amendment sets out the rules of the common law.

The eighth amendment protects the citizen against cruel and unusual punishments.

The ninth amendment ensures that the rights that are not enumerated in the Constitution are secure.

The tenth and final amendment limits the power of federal government by reserving for the states all powers that are not granted to the federal government by the Constitution.

I am sure you will agree that as good as the first ten amendments are, they are not very easy to reel off quickly, and in my opinion it would be beneficial to look at a much simpler statement of rights as well, in order to see how we could make our own bill of rights informative, but concise at the same time. For this purpose we could do a lot worse than to look at the Four Freedoms speech given by Franklin Roosevelt. It plainly states that there should be four fundamental freedoms that all persons on earth should enjoy. These are:

Freedom of speech
Freedom of worship
Freedom from want
Freedom from fear

These are rather simplistic, but as they are so simple it is easy for them to be recited by even the most uneducated person, and it would perhaps be safe to say that the reasons why they are correct could also be understood by all as well. It is obvious that they are rather too simple to be put down on paper and accepted by all, and if they were, there would be too much scope for widely differing interpretations. I think it would be proper to say that our own bill of rights would be better off halfway between the two examples that we have just looked at, with language plain enough to be understood by all, but with speech that would be fitting of the country that calls the great English language its own.

Although, as I have already stated, a complete bill of rights that would be legally sound is beyond my ability to set down, it is nonetheless important to examine perhaps one right in detail, as in effect the others all stem from the first. I am talking of course about the right of free speech. It is impossible to think of any other right that would come before this one in terms of its relevance and importance to every day life, and the ability of the people to feel safe, not just from attacks on them from the government, but from all other quarters as well. Perhaps the ultimate debate surrounding free speech has always been among those people who are religious, but also those who are irreligious. If people wish to be religious, and to go to religious institutions, and to go to religious services, and to interact with other religious people, then that is perfectly fine, and a secular democratic republic would allow this by definition. However, for the right to hold true for all people, they must not enjoin the rest of society to pay, in any way, for those institutions, or try and force their views onto other people. In addition, if any of their religious customs infringe on existing laws, such as genital mutilation of children for example, then they would not and should not be allowed to plead a religious excuse. In addition, persons who wish to be non-religious must not be interfered with by the state, and they also must not try and get their own personal views imposed on others. To make this as plain as can be the bill of rights must be godless, and governmental policy must derive from evidence, as that is the only common ground that both believers and non-believers have.

There is a reason why the first amendment to the U.S constitution is that of protecting freedom of speech. Free speech must extend to include the right to offend, and the right to criticise any idea no matter how sacredly it is held. I am paraphrasing much better minds than my own when I say that someone who attempts to stifle the free speech of another person is not just stopping that person from saying what they want, they are stopping themselves from having the means of changing their own minds. This feeling is so strong in the United States that there is in fact a group of people that describe themselves as First Amendment absolutists. If I was an American citizen I would undoubtedly be amongst their number, if only for the obvious reasons that freedom of speech must be utter and absolute. It is my belief, and many other peoples as well, that the first amendment is the most important one of them all, as without the freedom of speech, freedom of expression, freedom of association, and freedom of and from religion, then it is impossible for other freedoms and rights to follow. It is true that there are regular attacks on this amendment, especially in the form of religious disputes, but this would happen even if the language of the amendment was as perfectly and tightly written as any human statement could be. I certainly could not improve on the first amendment, limited as my intellect and lexicon is, but I do think that it could do with being broken up, as to be clearer and at less risk of being interpreted in a way that was not intended by the authors.

Perhaps the most famous example of an attempt to limit freedom of speech is that of the Justice Oliver Wendell Holmes, when, in asked what circumstance it would be proper to limit free speech, gave the example of shouting fire in a crowded theatre. What Holmes did not conclude was that you would be just as liable to start a panic if there was a fire and you did not shout fire, or if there was a fire and you did shout fire. It is also forgotten what he was speaking against, which in that case was the production of a leaflet, in Yiddish, by a group of Yiddish speaking socialists, who were opposed to the war and whose leaflet urged people not to sign up for it. They were jailed simply for producing the leaflet and writing about the event. Many people hold Holmes up as the person of merit in that case, but it should be crystal clear that there is no man or woman that has ever been born, or ever will be, that knows in advance what will constitute an offensive or inoffensive piece of writing, speech, art, or film. To have a law that claims that certain things must be offensive is to say that there has to be such a person.

Offence taking is a large part of the attempt, by some at any rate, to think that speech can be and should be limited, but this again is simply not the case. Most of the people who claim to be offended by certain pieces of writing, speech, ideas, or anything else, are the types of people who will go out of their way to be offended, no matter how careful you are to avoid causing any offence. In these cases there is nothing really that can be done, as if that person is determined to go out of their way to be offended, then there is no action or statement that you could not do or utter that would not end up causing offence.

Coming back to our situation in the constitutional monarchy in which we live, the right of freedom of speech, and especially the right to free speech which might and indeed may be designed to offend is doubly important, if only because of the deference that has been paid to just one institution and family in our long history. This is not to say that anyone that criticises the royals is hunted down or thrown into jail; to the contrary, there are many television and radio shows that satirise the monarchy, and there are and will be many more in the future. However, it is still rare to hear personal attacks on individual royals, even if they deserve the attack, and there lies under the edifice of our culture an unwillingness on most peoples part to openly criticise the monarchic system or institution. The ability to do this openly and to not have a taboo associated with it is one of the ideas that we must try and disseminate, especially if the action of moving to a republic relies, as I insist that it does, on the mindset of the people, and not those of the establishment or those few who hold most of the power.

Whatever shape or form our future bill of rights takes, it is pedantically obvious that it must include all of the major points that I have covered and examined in this chapter. These are namely the freedom to think, speak, and worship or not worship, and not have these actions infringed upon by the government, the ability to feel safe on their property and person, and the right to a fair trial. Other rights may be included as the need arises, but it is clear to any thinking person that a successful society must have the ones I have mentioned as an absolute bare minimum.

CONCLUSION

A republic if you can keep it

The power to mould the future of the Republic will be in the hands of the journalists of future generations.

- Joseph Pulitzer

If you have read thus far and I have managed to persuade you to change your stance with regards to the monarchy, it may upset you to know that even if we did achieve what many of us are setting out to achieve, which is the abolishment of the monarchy and the drafting of a constitution and a bill of rights, that will not be the end of the battle. We only have to look to the example of the United States to see that the constitutional edifice that the founding fathers built comes under attack even to this day from enemies both within the government and outside it. In the U.S there are forces at work that seek to teach the nonsense that is creationism in schools, to have a national day of prayer, presumably Christian, to have chaplains in the armed forces, to limit free speech, and to try and tear down much of the progress that they have made, both in terms of social and moral advancements. I do not think it would be unfair to say that the same would happen in our potential future democratic secular republic, and to understand this all we need do is look at recent events that have happened within our own borders. Plays and theatre productions have been picketed and threatened with closure - the Jerry Springer Opera being perhaps the most famous example of this - and even Geert Wilders, a Dutch filmmaker, was arrested at a London airport and deported back to Holland for producing a film that portrayed the plight of muslim women in his own country. The attack on free speech and free expression is perhaps the most worrying aspect of this, and the most dangerous part of the process is that it happens very slowly, with the freedom to say what you want eroded almost so imperceptibly as to be unnoticeable. Sooner or later though this right will be taken away from you, and then it will be too late to complain.

It is my strong opinion that the journalistic profession in this country needs to strive to reach a higher standard, in order to combat the very real threat of the people becoming too ignorant to do anything about their own situation. Too often the questions that should have been asked by the very people whose job it is to ask them have and do remain silent on important issues of the day. The false premise that respect must automatically be afforded to certain people or to certain arguments has to be demolished, or otherwise, as I stated earlier, it will become illegal to even have an opinion on a subject. Our laws of libel and slander do not help this matter, nor does the inculcation that certain groups of people are more right than others, or are more valuable than others by virtue of their birth, or that the class system is a rigid box in which people cannot climb out of or escape from.

If it turns out that the journalistic profession cannot be trusted completely to ask the questions that need to be asked of the men and women we put in power, and of the people themselves, then we must strive to train future generations to do the job in their place. No tyranny was ever allowed to rise with the consent of an educated and informed population, and it is in the young that this education must take place. The young do not have any preconceived notions of anything, especially the action of awarding respect to those who do not deserve it.

As I have said before, our ability to reason is perhaps the only thing that distinguishes us from the rest of the animal kingdom, and to ignore this fact, or to extinguish it, or to condemn it, or to criticise it, seems in my opinion absurd to the highest degree. We must protect this candle from all attempts of sabotage, for if we do not, then we lose that which is most precious about ourselves.

In closing, it is clear from all of the arguments, that one thing cannot be more certain, and that is that the status quo is not desirable. It is undesirable not just for the millions of people who are content to be labelled subjects, but also for the small number of mammals trapped within the institution itself. The sooner that we acknowledge that there are no special humans, or even more fantastically, divinely appointed ones, then our species will be able to start the long climb out of the mire of superstition and ignorance that we currently find ourselves in. The humans of five to ten thousand years in the future will have no time for superstition and deference to a person who was simply born into a position of alleged power, and there is no good reason why we should either.

Long live the republic.

Printed in Great Britain
by Amazon

40143474R00102